A Commentary on "Ecumenism: The Vision of the ELCA"

# A Commentary on
## *"Ecumenism:*
## *The Vision of the ELCA"*

William G. Rusch, editor

**AUGSBURG**     **MINNEAPOLIS**

Cover design: Eric Walljasper
Typesetting: Peregrine Publications

Library of Congress Cataloging-in-Publication Data

A Commentary on "Ecumenism: the vision of the Evangelical Lutheran Church in America" / edited by William G. Rusch.
   p.   cm.
   Includes bibliographical references.
   ISBN 0-8066-2515-5 (alk. paper)
   1. Evangelical Lutheran Church in America. Ecumenism.  2. Evangelical Lutheran Church in America–Relations.  3. Lutheran Church–Relations.  4. Evangelical Lutheran Church in America–Doctrines.  5. Lutheran Church–Doctrines.  6. Church–Unity.  7. Ecumenical movement.  8. Christian union.  I. Rusch, William G.  II. Evangelical Lutheran Church in America. Ecumenism.
   BX8063.7.A1C65  1990
   284.1'35–dc20                         90-34961
                                       CIP

The paper used in this publication meets the minimum requirements of American National Standard for Information Sciences–Permanence of Paper for Printed Library Materials, ANSI Z329.48-1984.

Manufactured in the U.S.A.                                 AF 9-2515

94    93    92    91    90    1    2    3    4    5    6    7    8    9    10

# Contents

# Foreword

The Office for Ecumenical Affairs has produced this volume, *A Commentary on Ecumenism: The Vision of the Evangelical Lutheran Church in America*. I hope this commentary on an important statement of our church, adopted by our first churchwide assembly as a working document, will be an aid to individuals within the Evangelical Lutheran Church in America and beyond who wish to study *Ecumenism*.

The ecumenical heritage of the predecessor church bodies of the Evangelical Lutheran Church in America was rich and deeply rooted in their history. Our challenge is to be faithful to this legacy and to give expression to the ecumenical stance of our church in this day and for the future. The Evangelical Lutheran Church in America is in the process of carrying out a churchwide study of *Ecumenism: The Vision of the Evangelical Lutheran Church in America* in order for the church to articulate its ecumenical vision in a responsible and creditable manner.

This commentary facilitates this process of study and reflection by providing a discussion, in greater detail than is possible in the text of *Ecumenism*, of the leading ideas in the statement and the rationale for their inclusion. I believe that this volume will assist our church in coming to a better understanding of its ecumenical potential and responsibility.

Herbert W. Chilstrom
Bishop

# Preface and Acknowledgments

Even prior to the formation of the Evangelical Lutheran Church in America (ELCA) on January 1, 1988, the Church Council agreed in October 1987 to a proposal from the Office for Ecumenical Affairs that a statement on ecumenism be developed for presentation to the first Churchwide Assembly in 1989.

This statement was to build upon the documents and commitments of the predecessor church bodies, as well as upon the constitution of the ELCA, and to offer a clear articulation of the scriptural, confessional, and constitutional foundations of this church for ecumenism; a description of the ecumenical heritage of the ELCA; and a declaration of ecumenical commitment.

The Office for Ecumenical Affairs, through its Standing Committee and staff, produced several drafts of a text in 1988 and 1989. These were shared at appropriate stages with congregations, college and seminary faculties, the Conference of Bishops, and other interested persons within this church. At the same time, a draft of the statement was given to several ecumenical organizations and churches with which the ELCA was in dialogue. In the production of a text for the Churchwide Assembly, all the submitted responses and critiques were carefully considered, and many were incorporated.

Upon the approval of the Standing Committee of the Office for Ecumenical Affairs and the Church Council, the final text of *Ecumenism: The Vision of the Evangelical Lutheran Church in America* was presented to the Churchwide Assembly in August 1989. The Assembly took the following action:

To adopt "Ecumenism: The Vision of the Evangelical Lutheran Church in America" as a working document, meaning it is

1. to offer provisional and interim guidance for this church during the 1990-91 biennium;
2. to be reviewed, studied, and discussed throughout this church during the 1990-91 biennium; and
3. to lead to presentation of a revised statement for action by the 1991 Churchwide Assembly.

Now the ELCA has the opportunity to continue to study this working document and to make recommendations for any revisions to be considered in the statement presented to the 1991 Assembly.

During this biennium the Office for Ecumenical Affairs is facilitating the review and study of *Ecumenism: The Vision of the Evangelical Lutheran Church in America* in several ways. This volume represents one of these efforts. The executive staff of the office has produced this commentary on the working document so that it may be seen in the context of contemporary Lutheran scholarship and the results of the modern ecumenical movement.

This commentary does not address each line in the text of the statement. Rather, it proceeds section by section with a discussion of the leading ideas in each. In this way it shows how the teachings of *Ecumenism: The Vision of the Evangelical Lutheran Church in America* are in harmony with Lutheran theology and the emerging consensus of the ecumenical movement.

Within the short time available, this commentary could not have been written without the special efforts of a number of individuals and ecumenical institutes. These include my colleagues in the Office for Ecumenical Affairs, Thomas F. Livernois, Daniel F. Martensen, Darlis J. Swan, and Karen M. Ward, and the Washington (D.C.) Institute of Ecumenics and the Institute for Ecumenical Research in Strasbourg. The research professors at Strasbourg have produced the position paper on Article VII of the Augsburg Confession and full communion that appears as an appendix. A special word of appreciation is owed to the ecumenical representative of the Metropolitan Washington, D.C., Synod, Scott S. Ickert, who did considerable research for the material in this volume, and to Toni Teplitz and Delene Hays, without whose efforts this book could not have been edited and produced so promptly. The Institute for Ecumenical Research at Strasbourg has also prepared a document entitled *Communio/Koinonia* that was published for the delegates at the Eighth Assembly of the Lutheran World Federation in Curitiba, Brazil. With the kind permission of the Institute, this document is printed in this volume as Appendix 2.

This commentary is intended to be a resource to aid those interested in the ecumenical stance of the ELCA to see in this working document an expression of ecumenical commitment in conformity with the teaching of Scripture and the Lutheran Confessions, and representative of the present stage of the ecumenical movement.

William G. Rusch
Executive Director
Office for Ecumenical Affairs

# Introduction

**The Evangelical Lutheran Church in America (ELCA) seeks in its faith and life "to manifest the unity given to the people of God by living together in the love of Christ and by joining with other Christians in prayer and action to express and preserve the unity which the Spirit gives" (ELCA Constitution 4.02.f.). In what follows, authoritative sources are first surveyed as a basis for the ecumenism of "joining with other Christians." Then, a history of Lutheran ecumenical experience is sketched to suggest continuity with predecessor churches.**

The Evangelical Lutheran Church in America affirms in its constitution that this church will seek "to manifest the unity given to the people of God by living together in the love of Christ and by joining with other Christians in prayer and action to express and preserve the unity which the Spirit gives" (4.02.f.). In their Sunday worship service, members of the ELCA pray: "For the peace of the whole world, for the well-being of the Church of God, and for the unity of all, let us pray to the Lord. Lord, have mercy."[1] The constitutional clause and the liturgical prayer are indications of the way in which the quest for Christian unity, "That they may all be one" (John 17:21), inspires the faith and shapes the life of the ELCA.

This ecumenical quest means more to the ELCA than the establishment of friendships among Christians or a sympathetic and tolerant understanding of other churches. This church lives by the unity that the Spirit of God gives. The ELCA is an expression of Lutheran unity in that it brings together three predecessor church bodies. It understands the joy and the challenge

13

of the ecumenical adventure. The experience of table fellowship, common witness, and a shared faith in the creative Word of God among the three churches motivated them to unite. The Spirit of God gives unity to the church, and the ELCA participates in that unity and is a visible expression of it.

By its own faith and life the ELCA clearly intends to be a sign of unity, but it also seeks to be a leaven for the unity of the church. The present church will join "with other Christians in prayer and action" (4.02.f.); it will celebrate and share with others what the Lord has done for the church and for the world in Jesus Christ. The ELCA will actively seek opportunities to unite with others in prayers of thanksgiving and intercession; to explore the faith and the hope that God gives to the church; to gather at the table of the Lord, breaking the bread of communion and drinking from the cup of salvation; and to bring to the world at large the covenant love and divine mercy that the one God and Father has revealed in the life, death, and resurrection of his Son, Jesus Christ.

To state the vision of the ELCA is to state an ecumenical vision, one that includes the full scope of God's redemptive creativity. This church first draws its courage from its triune confession of faith that the one God is the Lord of history, that Jesus Christ in his person and ministry is "the image of the invisible God, the first-born of all creation" (Col. 1:15). This church believes the Holy Spirit will lead both the church and the world "into all the truth" (John 16:13). The ELCA confidently proclaims the gospel (*evangelium*) of God's redemption in Christ "not only in word but also in power and in the Holy Spirit and with full conviction" (1 Thess. 1:5).

In the second place, this church can look to its own history as a source for courage and strength in its mission to proclaim the unity God's Spirit gives. Just as the confession of God's redemption of the world in Christ is constitutive for the faith and life of this church, so too, the events of the sixteenth century remain a critical benchmark for its understanding of proclamation. The historical events that came to be known as the Reformation continue to inform the mission and witness of the ELCA. There can be no doubt but that the Spirit of God was at work for unity of the church in the work of the Reformers.

Gospel and history come together in the life of the church. The ELCA is no exception to this rule. In the proposed text, *Ecumenism: The Vision of the Evangelical Lutheran Church in America*, the ELCA seeks to be both a faithful witness to the gospel's gift of salvation and an effective one in carrying forward the historical Lutheran commitment to unity in the gospel. As a witness to the gospel, this statement draws its strength from the biblical affirmation that Jesus Christ is the main cornerstone of church unity (Eph. 2:20). The author teaches us that in Christ "the whole structure is joined together and grows into a holy temple in the Lord; in whom you also are built into it for a dwelling place of God in the Spirit" (Eph. 2:21-22). As a witness for furthering the Reformation's quest for unity based on the gospel, the statement acknowledges its historical context as both rich and promising. Prior to the formation of this church, its predecessor bodies, both officially and informally, engaged in ecumenical discussions, participated in ecumenical organizations, and undertook a wide range of ecumenical activities. The purpose of *Ecumenism: The Vision of the Evangelical Lutheran Church in America* is to gather and focus the contributions of the predecessor churches in order to present the ecumenical stance of the present church.

The statement is to be studied and reviewed in the dynamic context of what God's Spirit is doing in the world. Composed with the faith that God is moving us toward greater unity in Jesus Christ, the statement should now be thoroughly examined by the community being led by Christ's Spirit. The opportunity for shared reflection and deliberation in the church comes, we believe, as a gift of the Spirit, watching over the church and leading it to the heavenly Jerusalem. "Behold, the dwelling of God is with men. He will dwell with them, and they shall be his people, and God himself will be with them . . ." (Rev. 21:3).

## NOTE

1. *Lutheran Book of Worship*, Lutheran Church in America, The American Lutheran Church, The Evangelical Lutheran Church in Canada, the Lutheran Church – Missouri Synod (Minneapolis: Augsburg; Philadelphia: Board of Publication, Lutheran Church in America, 1978), 58.

# 1
## Scriptural Witness

For its participation in the ecumenical movement, the Evangelical Lutheran Church in America is dependent on its understanding of Scripture and the Lutheran Confessions as set forth in its Constitution.

### Scriptural Witness

The scriptural announcement of unity begins with the narrative of one God creating and ruling the whole universe and all peoples (Genesis 1-11). Psalmists and prophets call the whole earth and all nations to unite in worshiping, praising, and proclaiming the God of glory, righteousness, salvation, and blessing (Psalms 96-100, Isaiah 45:22-23, 55:1-5, 60:1-3).

The unity of God is the starting point and the ending point of significant New Testament passages, which speak about the unity of the church. In Ephesians 4, Paul's list "One Lord, one faith, one baptism" (v. 5) culminates in a doxological celebration of the "one God and Father of us all, who is above all and through all and in all" (v. 6). The purpose of ministry in all its variety (vv. 11-12) is to bring the church to unity of faith and knowledge of the Son of God (v. 13). It is, therefore, a ministry which must attend to issues of truth (vv. 14-15a), for growing in the unity in Christ (vv. 15b-16).

The prayer of Jesus for his disciples in John 17, on the eve of his death on the cross, clearly links unity with truth and mission. "Sanctify them in the truth; your word is truth" (v. 17) leads into "as you sent me into the world, so I have sent them into the world" (v. 18). Then Jesus prays "that they all may be one; even as you, Father, are in me, and I in you"

(v. 21a). The unity of the disciples depends on unity with God, as Jesus says to the Father, "that they may also be in us." And unity has its goal in mission "that the world may know that you have sent me" (v. 21b). As understood in Christ's prayer, unity is given to the church, not for the sake of the church, but that the church might give itself in mission to the world for the sake of the Gospel.

According to similar references in John, the disciples, one with Christ and one with each other, are branches on the vine which are to "bear much fruit" (15:5). There shall be "one flock" (10:16), when Jesus brings the "other sheep," because there is "one shepherd" who died "to gather into one" the scattered children of God (11:50-52).

The "one body" of which Colossians speaks (3:15), to which Christians are called, is, according to First Corinthians, Christ's body (1 Cor. 12:12), marked by varieties of gifts and many different members (1 Cor. 12:4-11, 14-31). Thus, when the writings in the New Testament are compared, a variety of expressions of unity and structures emerges. The New Testament reminds us, too, that disputes and divisions were to be found in the earliest period of the church's existence (e.g., Acts 6:1, 15:1-29; Gal. 2:1-16; 1 Cor. 1:10-17, 3:1-4). Indeed on several occasions divisive teachings and false teachers were condemned (e.g. Rom. 16:17; Phil. 3:2-20; 1 John 2:18-20, 4:1-4; 2 John; Jude).

Those who disrupt the unity of the church are held to be culpable as wrongdoers (Gal. 2:11-20), who need to return to the truth of the Gospel and faith in Christ as the essentials for Christian fellowship. Only in the Gospel can genuine unity be achieved. The Scriptures present a realistic picture of both the human proclivity toward disunity and the unity that is possible through oneness in Christ. The Bible tells us what God wills, and warns us of the ever present threats to a mutually accepting Christian fellowship. Then, as now, it is necessary to be reminded, "welcome one another, therefore, as Christ has welcomed you, for the glory of God" (Rom. 15:7).

The section of Scriptural Witness seeks to present, not exhaustively but succinctly, the basic intention of Scripture with respect to God's promise of, and call for, unity. Prior to the formation of the ELCA, both the American Lutheran Church (ALC) and Lutheran Church in America (LCA) were of one voice with regard to the scriptural witness to ecumenism. The LCA statement *Ecumenism: A Lutheran Commitment* (1982) in the section on scriptural foundations and the ALC statement *Ecumenical Perspective and Guidelines* (1985) agree verbatim in their presentation of Scriptures.[1]

Scripture witnesses to the rich and diverse unity God intends for the whole creation (Gen. 1-11). Beginning with the chosen people of Israel and encompassing all nations, the love of God assembles people in worship and praise. All peoples and nations are called to proclaim the one God of glory, righteousness, salvation, and blessing (Ps. 96-100; Isa. 45:22-23; 55:1-5; 60:1-3).

Although the Bible clearly speaks of unity as God's plan, purpose, and intention, it is impossible to discern therein a single or simple biblical blueprint for unity. There is no simple answer to the question of what it means to be the people of God. Rather, an understanding grows and develops as God covenants with Israel and the church in the course of history. Whether it be in the history of Israel or the church, patterns of ministry, theology, ethos, and structure vary, sometimes substantially.

The search for unity begins with the Old Testament.[2] Here one finds a story of divine blessing and human alienation, of estrangement and reconciliation, of brokenness and restored unity. God created the world for harmony and fruitfulness; the community of men and women was made to be obedient and joyful. God creates human beings to live in the communion of divine love and in fellowship with one another (Gen. 2). However, in the biblical narrative, the power of sin alienated Adam and Eve from each other and from their Creator. God punished Adam and Eve, but the divine love for sinners is such that God continues to care for and watch over even those who disobey (Gen. 3-4).

The building of the tower of Babel epitomized the hubris of a self-serving people, who said: "Come, let us build ourselves a city, and a tower with its top in the heavens, and let us make a name for ourselves, lest we be scattered abroad upon the face of the whole earth" (Gen. 11:4). Here was an attempt to construct a false unity based on pride and presumption; but the result was disorder and separation from God.

Yet God promised to create a nation through the covenant with Abraham. Through the people of Israel, God would bring the gift of unity and the blessing of salvation to the entire world. God promised Abraham: "by you all the families of the earth shall bless themselves" (Gen. 12:3). God also gave them the law with these words: "Hear, O Israel: The Lord our God is one Lord" (Deut. 6:4). Israel, in turn, was to be single-minded in its devotion to God and refrain from lusting after other gods. The covenant gave Israel its identity as it bound the nation to God, and God to the nation.

However, Israel was not always obedient to the law. God raised up the prophets to speak the word of God to a rebellious Israel, calling the people back to their vocation of unity and mission for the world. Thus, the Servant sings: "And now the Lord says, who formed me from the womb to be his servant, to bring Jacob back to him, and that Israel might be gathered to him . . . he says: 'It is too light a thing that you should be my servant to raise up the tribes of Jacob and to restore the preserved of Israel; I will give you as a light to the nations, that my salvation may reach to the end of the earth'" (Isa. 49:5-6).

The prophets proclaimed God's judgment and offered the promise of reconciliation to a remnant (Jer. 23:3; 31:7; Zeph. 3:12). This would be a sign and a witness to God's redeeming love for all of humanity (Ezek. 6:8-10). The part would stand for the whole, God's remnant in Israel for the entire community of nations. An unlikely few would be the sign of the promised future reign of God over all the people of the earth (cf. Isa. 10:20-23; 11:1-10).

This future reign is brought to light, finally and irrevocably, in the life, death, and resurrection of Jesus Christ. Christ is the ultimate unity of creation and redemption:

> He is the image of the invisible God, the first-born of all creation. . . . He is before all things, and in him all things hold together. He is the head of the body, the church; he is the beginning, the first-born from the dead. . . . For in him all the fulness of God was pleased to dwell, and through him to reconcile to himself all things, whether on earth or in heaven, making peace by the blood of his cross. (Col. 1:15, 17-20)

Those who are baptized and are incorporated into his death and resurrection (Rom. 6:5-11) live between the times of promise and fulfillment (Rom. 8:19-25) and witness to the coming unity of the whole creation in the redeeming work of Christ. "Therefore God has highly exalted him and bestowed on him the name which is above every name, that at the name of Jesus every knee should bow, in heaven and on earth and under the earth, and every tongue confess that Jesus Christ is Lord, to the glory of God the Father" (Phil. 2:9-11).

The church, which includes both Jews and Gentiles, is one in the covenant of baptism. The classic New Testament texts on the unity of the church are well known:[3] 1 Corinthians 1:10-30 (a warning against division and an admonition to be united in Christ, the only foundation); 1 Corinthians 12 (the unity of the spirit in a multiplicity of gifts, one body with many members); Galatians 3:27f. (all are one in Christ without distinction of race, social status, or sex); Romans 12:3-8 (one body, though many, members one of another); Acts 4:32 (the company of the believers are of one heart and soul); John 10:16 (one shepherd and one flock); John 17:20-26 (all are one like the Father and the Son). But often the extent and significance of the New Testament's teaching about the unity of the Christian community are not appreciated.[4]

Christian unity is both a gift and task[5] and has practical implications for the people of God with regard to their common witness in the world and to the world. The gift may be accepted with gratefulness and praise; but the task requires discipline, dedication, and effort. Here, as in every aspect of the church's life, Lutherans distinguish the righteousness of faith from the righteousness of works. Lutherans will avoid ecclesiastical triumphalism on the one hand and resignation to the status quo on the other. While the goal of unity cannot be assumed, ignored, or taken for granted, neither can it be achieved through human effort or maintained at the expense of the truth and purity of the gospel, without which there is no unity in the Spirit. As Luther said:

> Apart from faith, all doctrine and life separate and disunite mankind. . . . Therefore there is no god, no doctrine, no life, no means that produces unanimity other than this God with his agency of faith. This faith draws us all into the Spirit; there all things are harmonious, and all external differences disappear. This does not imply that no external differences remain; it merely means that the heart does not cling to these, that these do not set one person against the other.[6]

This church acknowledges both the scriptural warrant for the unity of the people of God and the legitimate concern to preserve and protect, at whatever cost, witness to the one truth, which is Christ (cf. John 14:6).[7]

The gift of unity is among the marks of the church that have been traditionally identified as one, holy, catholic, and apostolic. Unity is fundamental to the church's identity. The truth of the gospel cannot be discussed in isolation from the question of the church's essential unity in Christ. "God our Savior . . . desires all men to be saved and to come to the knowledge of the truth. For there is one God, and there is one mediator between God and men, the man Christ Jesus, who gave himself as a ransom for all" (1 Tim. 2:3-6). The true unity of the church is that which exists in Christ. The church is "one body" (Col. 3:15). "Because there is one bread, we who are many are one body, for we all partake of the one bread" (1 Cor. 10:17; cf. Rom. 6:3-5). Those who partake of the one body, which is Christ, are one body in him.

Christ breaks down the dividing walls of hostility, "that he might create in himself one new man in place of the two, so making peace, and might reconcile us both to God in one body through the cross" (Eph. 2:14-16). Christ takes former strangers and sojourners and makes them common members of the household of God (Eph. 2:19). The word of the cross is what unites the body "in the same mind and the same judgment" (1 Cor. 1:10). As the church is united with its Lord in the Eucharist and the word of the cross, so are its members united one to the other.

But the church does not exist unto itself. The extension of its witness in mission also depends on the origins of its unity. Jesus' glory is given to the church "that they may become perfectly one, so that the world may know that thou hast sent me" (John 17:23). The church's unity reaches beyond itself to include all those who are not a part of the household of faith; the church's unity in Christ is both the presupposition and the goal of its mission.

The one church and the one gospel do encounter resistance, even hostility; the one truth brings division. "Do you think that I have come to give peace on earth? No, I tell you, but rather division" (Luke 12:51). Evil, hatred, slander, and jealousy will remain in this world as long as "we still have the old Adam hanging around our necks."[8] The church must beware; false unity is actually disunity in disguise. Those who preach "another gospel" are accursed (Gal. 1:9), for the real outcome of their "works of the flesh" is dissension and party spirit (Gal. 5:19-20).

The unity of the church is a work of the Spirit of God, who unites all in Christian love.[9] If divine judgment brings division, it is to rebuild, to reform, and to reconcile. God destroys in order to make new. "I will give them one heart, and put a new spirit within them" (Ezek. 11:19, cf. 18:26). "And you shall be called by a new name which the mouth of the Lord will give" (Isa. 62:2b). "Once you were no people but now you are God's people . . ." (1 Pet. 2:10). As the people of God formed into one body through the agency of the Spirit, the saints are equipped by the Spirit to engage in battle against the temptations of the flesh (cf. Eph. 3:16; 6:17), temptations that lead inevitably to factionalism and disunity (cf. 1 Cor. 3). God does not abide a party spirit. "For those who are factious and do not obey the truth, but obey wickedness, there will be wrath and fury" (Rom. 2:8). Through baptism, however, all the faithful are initiated into the one eschatological community,[10] the new creation coming to fruition in Christ, but not yet here in its fullness (Isa. 65:17; 66:22; Gal. 6:15; 2 Pet. 3:13; Rev. 21:1). Though the faithful endure division and dissension, they persevere with hope in God's promise of unity and reconciliation. As Paul said concerning Israel: "For if their rejection means the reconciliation of the world, what will their acceptance mean but life from the dead?" (Rom. 11:15).

This new community is conceived in love, determined and guided by it. Love becomes the measure of its life. "God is love" (1 John 4:8). Here is the heart of the gospel's truth, with consequences for the life and mission of the community. "Beloved, let us love one another; for love is of God" (1 John 4:7). "Walk in love, as Christ loved us and gave himself up for us" (Eph. 5:2). "As the Father has loved me, so have I loved you; abide in my love" (John 15:9). "Beloved, if God so loved us, we also ought to love one another" (1 John 4:11). God's love in Christ means life, salvation, wholeness; these are gifts of the Spirit. Jesus is called "Emmanuel," which means "God with us" (Matt. 1:23). Christ, in union with the Father in the Spirit, binds himself in eternal solidarity to the new community, which is his own body. This gospel frees God's people to forbear one another in love, making them eager to "maintain the unity of the Spirit in the bond of peace" (Eph. 4:3). As Christ's love binds him to his people, this love overflows as believers extend his love in commitment and solidarity to the body for the sake of the whole world. The love of God, effective and concrete, i.e., incarnate in Jesus Christ,[11] is the very essence of the gospel. "For God so loved the world that he gave his only Son, that whoever believes in him should not perish but have eternal life. For God sent the Son into the world, not to condemn the world, but that the world might be saved through him" (John 3:16-17).

The church "possesses a variety of gifts, yet is united in love without sect or schism."[12] As love builds unity, it does not preclude diversity; in fact, it includes and celebrates it (1 Cor. 12:4-11, 14-31). For diversity complements and builds up. This is not the same as disunity, for disunity, which cannot tolerate diversity, tears down; and as it is the death of faith, so it is also the death of the Christian community (cf. Col 2:4-7; Acts 20:29-35).

The church in its various manifestations must strive for unity because its life is grounded in the unity that Christ and the Father enjoy. The church is one and must be one because they are one (John 17:20-24; 1 John 1:3). This unity is given from above and is not based on human affection or achievement; it is a gift and command of God (cf. 1 John 1:3; 4:7-12). God intends the community to be ever more inclusive; thus God's promise and command imply a reaching out. Unity has its goal in mission (John 17:21b).[13] This extension of the community is not coercion, neither is it simply mere uniformity. Never uniform, ever diverse, the church is always one. "The church" for the New Testament is always the local church and the universal church, the local community and the community of the whole, both of which are the one church, the one body of Christ.[14]

The unity of the church presupposes a multiplicity of churches in which there will not be a single form of worship, no uniform structures, or even a uniform theology.[15] Such diversity was already a feature of the New Testament church.[16] The church has been diverse since its beginning and will remain rich in variety until its mission has attained the perfection promised in Christ.[17] In Christ it is always united in diversity, for the church's confession of Christ is a confession of the *una sancta ecclesia*.[18]

A survey of the biblical literature yields one conclusion: one church with a richness of diversity in theology, worship forms, and structures that know tensions and disputes; but divisions and large numbers of Christians separated from full fellowship with one another are not to be found.[20]

## NOTES

1. See *Ecumenism: A Lutheran Commitment,* an official statement of the Lutheran Church in America adopted by the Eleventh Biennial Convention, Louisville, Kentucky, September 3-10, 1982 (New York: Lutheran Church in America, 1982) and *Ecumenical Perspective and Guidelines,* a paper prepared by the Standing Committee on Inter-Church Relations in response to the 1982 General Convention (Minneapolis: The American Lutheran Church, 1985), adopted as an official statement of the American Lutheran Church at the June 1985 meeting of the Church Council.

2. How this biblical material is seen in contemporary ecumenical literature may be observed in Paul A. Crow, Jr., *Christian Unity: Matrix for Mission* (New York: Friendship Press, 1982), 30-31; William G. Rusch, *Ecumenism: A Movement Toward Church Unity* (Philadelphia: Fortress Press, 1985), 1-8.

3. Johann Gamberoni, "Die Einheit des Volkes Gottes und der Kirche nach Zeugnis der Schrift – Altes Testament" and Franz Georg Untergassmair "Die Einheit des Volkes Gottes und der Kirche nach dem Zeugnis der Schrift – Die Einheit der Kirche en Neuen Testament," both in *Handbuch der Ökumenik, I,* ed. H.J. Urban and Howard Wagner (Paderborn: Bonifatius Verlag, 1985), 37-87. See also James Dunn, *Unity and Diversity in the New Testament* (Philadelphia: Trinity Press, 1989). See also Hans Küng, *The Church* (Garden City, NY: Image Books, 1976), 351-53. See also Eugene L. Brand, *Toward a Lutheran Communion: Pulpit and Altar Fellowship,* Lutheran World Federation (LWF) Report no. 26 (Geneva: Lutheran World Federation, 1988), 13-16. Brand especially highlights the Pauline and Johannine writings on the subject of *koinonia.*

4. Christian Link, Ulrich Luz, Lukas Vischer, *Sie aber hielten fest an der Gemeinshaft: Einheit der Kirche als Prozess in neuen Testament und heute* (Zurich: Benziger/Reinheit, 1988).

5. Cf. *Ecumenical Perspective and Guidelines* IV.1: "The unity of the church is a *gift,* given by God as part of that new community created by faith in the Gospel; the unity of the church is also a *task* as Christians and churches seek to manifest that which God has given."

6. Jaroslav Pelikan, ed., *Selected Psalms II,* vol. 13, *Luther's Works* (St. Louis: Concordia Publishing House, 1956), 7.

7. On Luther and the question of truth and unity, see Heiko Oberman, *Luther: Man Between God and the Devil* (New Haven: Yale University Press, 1989), 250: "Luther does not stand for the alternatives of 'truth not unity,' 'conscience not institution,' 'individual not community.' His declaration of loyalty to the Church as the communion of saints in the *Grosser Kathechismus* of 1529 should have ruled out such false alternatives. For the Church is 'unified in love, beyond factions and divisions.' As long as the Protestant tendency to play off the invisible Church of the

faithful against the visible institutional Church has not been overcome, this declaration will make no impression. These words are wrongly read as if Luther was thinking of the ideal Church, which can never and may never become real." Cf. this with the remarks of Harding Meyer, "Models of Unity," in *Vision: oikoumene* (Washington, D.C.: Washington Institute of Ecumenics, 1986), who speaks of a "counterproductive and ecumenically destructive principle," namely, "the opinion that ecumenical commitment and confessional loyalty, unity of the church and confessional identity are fundamentally opposed to each other and irreconcilable, and that, therefore, the unity of the church can only be achieved if the individual churches are giving up and abandoning their confessional identity."

8. Jaroslav Pelikan, ed., *Sermons on the Gospel of St. John: Chapters 1-4,* vol. 22, *Luther's Works* (St. Louis: Concordia Publishing House, 1957), 177.

9. See Bible study by Professor Claus Meister on 1 Corinthians 12:12-13 in *Unity in the Spirit – Diversity in the Churches: Report of the Conference of European Churches' Assembly VIII* (Geneva: Conference of European Churches, 1979), 30-31.

10. See William A. Norgren and William G. Rusch, eds., *Implications of the Gospel* (Minneapolis: Augsburg, 1988), 19-21.

11. See also *Auf dem Weg zu sichtbarer Einheit*, an agreement formulated at Meissen in 1988 by the Church of England, the Bund der Evangelischen Kirchen in der Deutschen Demokratischen Republik and the Evangelische Kirche in Deutschland (Berlin: Bund der Evangelischen Kirchen in der Deutschen Demokratischen Republik; Hannover: Evangelische Kirche in Deutschland, 1988), Section III, "Growth towards full, visible unity" is pertinent here: "In order to fulfill its mission the Church itself must be united. . . . This unity will reflect the different gifts God has given to his Church in many nations, languages, cultures and traditions. The unity we seek must at one and the same time respect these different gifts and manifest more fully the visibility of the one Church of Jesus Christ"(6). "Perfect unity awaits the final coming of God's Kingdom. . . . But in a fallen world we are committed to strive for the 'full, visible unity' of the body of Christ on earth. We are to work for that unity at every level. . . . All our attempts to describe this vision are bound to be provisional. We are continually being led to see fresh depths and riches of that unity and to grasp new ways in which it might be manifested in word and life"(7). "This 'full, visible unity' will include the following: a common confession of the apostolic faith in word and life; the sharing of one baptism, the celebrating of one eucharist and the service of a reconciled, common ministry; and 'bonds of communion' which enable the Church to interpret the apostolic faith, to take decisions, to teach authoritatively, to share goods and to bear effective witness in the world"(8).

12. Large Catechism in *The Book of Concord,* ed. Theodore G. Tappert (Philadelphia: Fortress Press, 1959), 65.

13. See John Mbiti, "An Ecumenical Approach to Teaching the Bible," in *The Teaching of Ecumenics,* ed. Samuel Amirtham and Cyris H.S. Moon (Geneva: World Council of Churches Publications, 1987), 33: "God's calling of Abraham (Abram) is for the sole purpose of executing the ecumenical outreach in the world. . . . There is a common beginning, an ecumenical beginning to creation, to humanity (in Adam

and Eve). There is also an ecumenical promise (covenant with Noah, with Abraham and on Sinai) which runs through the Old Testament. When we come to the New Testament, there is an ecumenical centre in Jesus Christ. He becomes the fulfillment of God's promise and at the same time the new promise for the completion of all things."

14. Ellen Flessman-van Leer, ed., *The Bible: Its Authority and Interpretation in the Ecumenical Movement*, Faith and Order Paper no. 99 (Geneva: World Council of Churches, 1980), 28: "In the fulfillment of their missionary task most churches claim not merely to be reproducing themselves, but in some sense to be planting the *una sancta ecclesia*. Surely this fact has implications which are scarcely yet realized, let alone worked out, both for the life of the mother churches, and also for all that is involved in the establishing of any new church in an ecumenical age. It demands that the liberty of newly-founded churches be recognized, so that both mother and daughter churches may receive together the one gift of God's grace. This demands faithfulness to the whole *koinonia* of Christ's Church, even when we are engaged with particular problems."

15. Küng, *The Church*, 355-56.

16. Küng, *The Church*, 35-41.

17. See Stephen Sykes, *The Identity of Christianity* (Philadelphia: Fortress Press, 1984), 18: "From the start there was a diversity of interpretations of Jesus' teaching." See also 21: "Disagreements which the writers of the New Testament had to en-counter are not accidental . . . it was the very nature of Christian Profession itself which provoked those disagreements. Internal conflict inheres in the Christian tradition, even in its earliest forms." And 29: "There is no dimension of Christianity which is not controversial."

18. See Karl Barth, *Church Dogmatics*, vol. 4 (Edinburgh: T. & T. Clark, 1956), 679: "The division [of the church] is a shame and a scandal, but this does not alter the fact that concretely the gathering to the community means for each of us the gathering of one of these divided communions. And it is not an acceptance of the scandal or an acquiescence in the shame if we say that we are not only permitted but commanded to start from this fact in our confession of the *una ecclesia*. All Churches and all the Christians united in them are called upon primarily to take themselves seriously even in their distinctness and therefore in their separate existence and confession – not necessarily to remain in them, and certainly not to harden in them but to reach out from them to the one Church."

19. Rusch, *Ecumenism*, 9.

# 2
## Lutheran Confessions

The concern for the unity of the church articulated in Scripture enjoyed considerable prominence in the first centuries of the history of the church. It was expressed in the Apostles' Creed and especially in the Nicene Constantinopolitan Creed of A.D. 381. These ecumenical symbols, along with the Athanasian Creed, were included in the Book of Concord in 1580. Their inclusion, as well as the first articles of the Augsburg Confession, show the desire of the Lutheran Reformers to identify with this biblical and patristic tradition.

The Lutheran Confessions were the products of an effort at evangelical reform, which, contrary to its intention, resulted in divisions within the Western church. As evangelical writings, they stress justification by grace through faith alone as the criterion for judging all church doctrine and life. As catholic writings, they assert that the Gospel is essential to the church being one, holy, catholic, and apostolic. They are concerned for the oneness of Christ's church under the Gospel, the preservation of the true catholic heritage, and the renewal of the church as a whole. That the Confessions have such concerns can be seen from the following:

1. They always point to Scripture, with its emphasis on one Lord and one church, as normative. It is not only the Scriptures' teaching on one Lord and one church that is pertinent here, but also their teaching on the truth of the Gospel, which they see as the only sufficient basis for Christian unity.
2. They begin with the ancient ecumenical creeds—Apostles', Nicene, and Athanasian—as "the three chief symbols." Lutherans always have

a common basis with those who share these creeds and the Bible.

3. They draw upon the reflection of the early church leaders in East and West, and thus share a common resource with those who also know and honor the theologians of the patristic era.

4. While many of the Lutheran Confessions were hammered out in the struggles of the sixteenth century and dwell on the differences with the Roman Catholics, the Reformed, the Anabaptists, and even some Lutherans, they also contained, whether specifically noted or not, many points of basic agreement with such groups.

5. The primary Lutheran confessional document, the Augsburg Confession of 1530, claims to be a fully catholic as well as evangelical expression of Christian faith. Part I, which lists the chief articles of faith, states that the Confession is grounded clearly in Scripture and does not depart from the universal Christian Church. The confessors at Augsburg asked only for freedom to preach and worship in accordance with the Gospel. They were willing, upon recognition of the legitimacy of these reforms, to remain in fellowship with those who did not share every theological formulation or reforming practice, e.g., Augsburg Confession, Preface, Article XV, Article XXVIII and Conclusion. It is in this historical context that Article VII is to be understood: "for the true unity of the church it is enough (*satis est*) to agree concerning the teaching of the Gospel and the administration of the sacraments."

The historical situation is now different. The question is no longer that of preserving an existing church unity, but that of reestablishing a communion (fellowship, *communio*), which has suffered many breaks. The considerable difference in situation between 1530 and today needs to be noted carefully. In 1530, the primary challenge was to preserve church unity in the Western church and recover the proclamation of the Gospel from various abuses. Today a major challenge is to move from disunity toward greater expressions of unity among divided churches. The *satis est* could function differently in a context of threatened disunity in comparison to the present situation of visible disunity. In a context of unity the *satis est* was proposed to preserve that unity. Today the *satis est* provides an ecumenical resource to move to levels of fellowship among divided churches. Article VII for all its cohesiveness and precision does not present a complete doctrine of the church. It is not in the first instance an expression of a falsely understood ecumenical openness and freedom from church order, customs, and usages in the church. Its primary meaning is that only those things that convey salvation, justification by grace through faith, are allowed to be signs and constitutive elements of the church. It is also necessary to recognize the missionary situation of the global church in our time, which did not exist in the 16th century.

Yet Article VII of the Augsburg Confession continues to be ecumenically freeing, because of its insistence that agreement in the Gospel suffices for Christian unity. As Lutherans seek to enter into fellowship without insisting on doctrinal or ecclesiastical uniformity, they place an ecumenical emphasis on common formulation and expression of theological consensus on the Gospel. There is room for living and experiencing fellowship within the context of seeking larger theological agreement.

6. Other Lutheran confessional documents, though differing in nature and purpose from each other, are consistent with the Augsburg Confession on church unity. For example:

a. The Small Catechism teaches in a simple form the evangelical and catholic faith, so that this faith may be known by all the people of God.

b. The Formula of Concord of 1577 reflects, in detail, inner Lutheran theological debate and disagreement, and suggests, in spite of its emphasis on rejection and condemnation of errors and contrary doctrine, the possibility of resolving and reconciling differences "under the guidance of the Word of God."

Rooted in this biblical and confessional understanding as stated in its Confession of Faith (ELCA Constitution, Chapter 2), the Evangelical Lutheran Church in America identifies itself with this vision of a greater wholeness of Christ's people.

Chapter 4 of the constitution, "Statement of Purpose," declares that the commitment of the Evangelical Lutheran Church in America is both to Lutheran unity and to Christian unity (4.03.d. and 4.03.f.).

The understanding of ecumenism in the Evangelical Lutheran Church in America embraces more than Lutheran denominations. This church rejoices in the movement toward agreement with other churches. The degree of openness on the part of others and our own confessional commitment have a bearing upon the developing relations and growth in unity with "all those who in every place call on the name of our Lord Jesus Christ, their Lord and ours" (1 Cor. 1:2).

The articulation and the shape of the church's unity is normed by Scripture; but also, in a derivative sense, by creed and confession. *The Book of Concord* (1580) includes among its first articles the three chief ecumenical symbols, the Apostles', Nicene-Constantinopolitan, and Athanasian Creeds.[1] The statement that the Lutherans wanted to make to the rest of the church was clear: The Lutheran movement did not see itself as a sect, but as an evangelical movement within the Western catholic tradition.[2] "We have introduced nothing, either in doctrine or ceremonies, that is contrary to Holy Scripture or the universal Christian church."[3] "We on our part shall not omit doing anything, insofar as God and conscience allow, that may serve the cause of Christian unity."[4]

The Lutheran movement knew itself as a distinctive witness for the truth of the gospel. The Lutheran Confessions were the result of efforts for evangelical reform, to clarify and articulate that which stands at the very center of the Christian faith. "The Lutheran proposal of dogma has one great and central theme: justification by faith alone apart from works of law."[5] The foundation and cornerstone of the Lutheran confessional witness was proposed, not as one doctrine among others, but as the hermeneutical key to unlock the truth of all Christian theology, Scripture, and confession. This is not merely a method of reiterating correct words and phrases. It is not enough simply to repeat the words "justification," "faith," and "grace." Justification by faith not only provides the necessary context for grace, it also indicates the source, the means, and the recipient of grace. For example, it would have been difficult to find a representative of the scholastic traditions – Pelagians, Luther called them – who would have disagreed with the proposition that salvation is by grace through faith. The doctrine of justification governs the way one speaks or interprets the Word of God. Justification might better be referred to as a "metalinguistic stipulation" – governing all evangelical witness, reflection, and proclamation.[6]

The Lutheran Confessions bear witness to the gospel. It is on this basis alone that the church is one. The true catholic heritage, which the confessions seek to preserve and defend, and the renewal of the church as a whole, are not incompatible or mutually exclusive goals. Each is to be tempered by the other. This can be seen from the following:

1. Scripture, according to the confessions, is the only rule and norm. "We believe, teach, and confess that the prophetic and apostolic writings of the Old and New Testaments are the only rule and norm according to which all doctrines and teachers alike must be appraised and judged."[7] However, Scripture teaches that there is one Lord and one church, which "will be and remain forever."[8]

The goal of ecclesiastical and confessional unity does not obviate diversity; and this diversity does not compromise the singular truth of the gospel. Still, the confessions demand that agreement on the gospel is the only basis for Christian unity. What the confessions have in mind is the unity of the church and not an association of like-minded people bonded together by mutual attraction or affection. That the church is one means that it is united in faith, despite its necessary and characteristic diversity. The existence and identity of the church is based solely on the gospel. "Outside the Christian church (that is, where the Gospel is not) there is no forgiveness, and hence no holiness. All who seek to merit the forgiveness of sin through their works rather than through the Gospel and the forgiveness of sin have expelled and separated themselves from the church."[9] This church, whose differences are both confirmed and transcended by the gospel, is characterized by its oneness in the faith: "I believe that there is on earth a little holy flock or community of pure saints under one head, Christ. It is called together by the Holy Spirit in one faith, in love without sect or schism."[10]

2. Lutherans accept the three chief symbols, and acknowledge a common basis with other Christians who share the ecumenical creeds, i.e., those who maintain the truth of the gospel as it has been handed down in the ancient formulas and confession of the faith. Unity is to be acknowledged and achieved on the basis of a common faith in, and confession of, the Triune God.

Ecumenical advancement can only be achieved on the basis of this common confession. The three ecumenical creeds are springboards to unity, but they also provide the limits and boundaries to what may be considered proper evangelical witness to the one faith in the one Lord Jesus Christ. Where there is a common confession of faith and a common witness to the Triune God, the door is open to greater forms of visible unity. One cannot speak about the true unity of the church of Jesus Christ where such common witness and confession are not possible.

3. The confessions draw upon the wisdom and insight of the leaders of the early church, both East and West, thereby witnessing to a common heritage and making use of a common resource shared by all who acknowledge the patristic contribution to the Christian tradition. Clearly the authority of the "Fathers" is not to be placed alongside that of Scripture. "Other writings of ancient and modern teachers, whatever their names, should not be put on a par with Holy Scripture. Every single one of them should be subordinated to the Scriptures."[11] Moreover, there is a variety of opinions among them; they often erred and could be deceived.[12] Still the confessions regularly appeal to their authority.[13] Melanchthon also viewed the "Fathers" as important sources of interpretive insight. Even though they often erred, their perception into the meaning of the biblical text was frequently insightful, evangelical, and illuminating.[14]

4. The Lutheran Confessions do not condemn other Christians, only specific doctrines that are proved false by Scripture. For example, Lutherans

disagreed with Rome over the nature of Christ's presence in the Eucharist, but Lutherans acknowledged a common tradition of faith in the real presence. Though the confessions also denied that bishops rule by divine right, the Reformers nevertheless stated their willingness to accept the authority of bishops in spiritual matters provided such authority is exercised by human right. While Melanchthon states that "it is plain that the marks of the Antichrist coincide with those of the pope's kingdom and his followers,"[15] Melanchthon also conceded that if the pope would allow the gospel, "we, too, may concede to him that superiority over the bishops which he possesses by human right."[16]

In 1529, at Marburg, Lutheran and Reformed leaders were gathered together at the invitation of Philip of Hesse in order to iron out their differences. Agreement was achieved on all articles but one. Luther wrote to his wife that we are "of one opinion in almost everything." He added, "at the Lord's Supper, however, they will allow bread to be only physically and Christ to be only spiritually present. . . . I suppose that God has blinded them."[17] Issues related to the real presence and the implications this has for Christology have divided Lutherans and Reformed to this day. Yet, already in the sixteenth century a considerable convergence was evident in many important matters, including such fundamental issues as ecclesiology and justification.[18]

The Anabaptists drew considerable scorn and criticism from the confessions. The Augsburg Confession in particular attempted to show common cause with Rome over against those whom Luther termed "fanatics." The Formula of Concord claims that the Anabaptists "profess doctrines of a kind that cannot be tolerated either in the church, or in the body politic."[19] Yet it was the Anabaptists who stressed, if one-sidedly, that Christian unity depends only on the working of the Spirit; and that the truth of what they considered the gospel must be upheld at all costs.

5. The Augsburg Confession of 1530 claims to be a fully catholic as well as evangelical expression of Christian faith. It claims to be grounded in Scripture and that its confession in no way departs from the fundamental teachings of the universal church. "We have introduced nothing, either in doctrine or in ceremonies, that is contrary to Holy Scripture or the universal Christian church."[20] Part I concludes with an appeal for leniency on the part of the bishops, "even if there were some defect among us in regard to traditions . . . there is nothing unfounded or defective in the principal articles."[21] The dissension is concerned with certain abuses that had crept into the church. "There is nothing here that departs from the Scriptures or the catholic church or the church of Rome."[22]

Note that a distinction is made here between the "catholic church" and the "church of Rome." In neither case do the Lutherans claim to have departed from the principal formulations of faith common to both. The catholic church that the Lutherans confess to be a part of is more than just the church of Rome. The catholic church is a matter of grace, faith, and confession of Word and sacrament. Luther often stated that the church is not a juridical organization, but the assembly of believers.[23] Here is a bond of unity that transcends law and human ceremonies. It is on the basis of grace, faith, and confession that the church's unity depends. It is on this foundation, and this foundation alone, that the Lutherans claim to be one with the church of Rome in the catholic church.

The confessor at Augsburg asked only for freedom to preach and worship in accordance with the gospel. "Our churches do not ask that the bishops should restore peace and unity at the expense of their honor and dignity (though it is incumbent on the bishops to do this, too, in case of need), but they ask only that the bishops relax certain unreasonable burdens which did not exist in the church in former times and which were introduced as contrary to the custom of the universal Church."[24] "It is not our intention to find ways of reducing the bishops' power, but desire and pray that they may not coerce our consciences to sin."[25]

The framers of the Augsburg Confession (CA) were willing, upon recognition of the legitimacy of reforms, to remain in fellowship with those who did not share every theological formulation or reforming practice, e.g., Preface, Articles XV and XXVIII, and the Conclusion. With regard to church usages that have been established by men, "it is taught among us that those usages are to be observed which may be observed without sin and which contribute to peace and good order in the church" (Art. XV).

It is in this historical context that CA VII is to be understood, for it does not require that "ceremonies, instituted by men, be observed uniformly in all places."[26] The historical situation we find ourselves in today is vastly different from that of the sixteenth century. The question is no longer that of preserving an existing church unity, but of reestablishing a communion (fellowship, *communion*), which has suffered many breaks.[27] The Lutheran Confessions provide a necessary basis for Lutheran churches seeking evangelical unity as they work to overcome the persistent and scandalous disunity of the body of Christ. The confessions offer a basis for unity in the Spirit through Word and sacrament, confessional unity as *communion in sacris*.[28]

In the sixteenth century the catholic church was rent asunder because the church of Rome employed coercive measures against the free proclamation of the gospel. Today, after centuries of division and mutual condemnation, the church struggles to give the gospel a common voice. Then disunity was an unfortunate and temporary necessity in order to preserve the gospel's integrity; today the achievement of the church's unity is necessary in order to accomplish the same goal. Then the one truth was not to be suppressed; now the one truth is in danger of being divided or compromised. Then an emergency situation demanded drastic action; now that the emergency has passed it is incumbent on divided Christians that a healing process begin. Today's theological and structural pluralism must not ossify our present disunity. CA VII inspires new approaches to ecumenism: "It is sufficient (*satis est*) for the true unity of the Christian church that the Gospel be preached in conformity with a pure understanding of it and that the sacraments be administered in accordance with the divine Word."

Article VII does not present a complete doctrine of the church. Instead it rather self-consciously sets out the requirements, or basis for church unity. No additional requirements for unity need be considered constitutive; however, the creation of models of unity is required. The development of these models is in no way intended to bring to an end or complete the many efforts and plans for achieving unity; it is, rather, the evangelical foundation upon which many diverse structures and "ceremonies" may be built.[29]

Since the sixteenth century, new challenges have helped us appreciate the freedom permitted by Article VII. For example, the missionary situation of the global church in our time did not exist in the sixteenth century; cooperation is now demanded of us for the sake of the gospel. Many forces are contending against the gospel today, and our divided, competing efforts at evangelism only frustrate and unnecessarily complicate the church's universal mission. More than practical necessity or mere efficiency is at stake. Cooperation is a necessity for mission so that the integrity of the gospel might be preserved. "We should not consider as matters of indifference . . . ceremonies which are basically contrary to the Word of God."[30] Since the emergency situation of the sixteenth century has passed, a persistent disunity is contrary to the Word of God; new challenges confront the church in our time.

Article VII is freeing, for it permits confessional Lutheranism to seek fellowship without insisting on doctrinal or ecclesiastical uniformity, while at the same time striving to achieve common formulation and expression of theological consensus on the gospel. "The primary requirement for basic and permanent concord within the church is a summary formula and pattern, unanimously approved, in which the summarized doctrine commonly confessed by the churches of the pure Christian religion is drawn together out of the Word of God."[31] Article VII reminds the church of what is basic to its confession and life. It is on this basis that the church is free to formulate statements of confessional consensus.[32] CA VII opens up a process of conversation, debate, experimentation, and even action leading to the formation of structures, albeit provisional, as a result of which the unity of the church may be realized more fully.

6. Luther's Small Catechism is fully consistent with the Augsburg Confession concerning the unity of the church. The unity of the church, its very existence, does not depend on human structures, not even on pure doctrine, but on the gift of the Spirit: "The Holy Spirit has called me through the Gospel, enlightened me with his gifts, and sanctified and preserved me in true faith, just as he calls, gathers, enlightens, and sanctifies the whole Christian church on earth and preserves it in union with Jesus Christ in the one true faith."[33] This "one true faith" is the response to Word and sacrament and not the ability to appropriate and formulate right doctrine.

The Formula of Concord states that Luther's catechisms contain everything that Scripture discusses at greater length.[34] This teaching is for all of God's people. It should not be forced on anyone, for this would only repeat the errors perpetrated by the Lutheran opposition. For example, concerning the sacrament: "You are not to make a law of this, as the pope has done. All you need to do is clearly to set forth the advantage and disadvantage, the benefit and loss, the blessing and danger connected with this sacrament. Then the people will come of their own accord and without compulsion on your part."[35]

The Formula of Concord of 1577 suggests the possibility of resolving and reconciling differences "under the guidance of the Word of God and the Comprehensive Summary of our Christian Teaching." Controversy arose among the Lutherans because some theologians departed from it in several important and significant articles, "either because they failed to grasp their true meaning or because they did not abide by them."[36] Others gave false interpretations of the Augsburg Confession, which precipitated schisms. These controversies, however, are not considered to be "mere misunderstandings or contentions about words"; rather, they "deal with weighty and important matters, and they are of such a nature that the opinions of the erring party cannot be tolerated in the church of God, much less be excused and defended."[37]

The framers of the Formula want to make it clear that it was not they who departed from Scripture, creeds, and the Lutheran confessional writings. These writings "have always and everywhere been accepted as the common and universally accepted belief of our churches, that the chief and most illustrious theologians of that time subscribed to them, and that all Evangelical churches and schools received them."[38] "It is the same simple, unchanging, constant truth," which is here confessed. "We do not, as our adversaries charge, veer from one doctrine to another. On the contrary, we want to be found faithful to the commonly accepted Christian meaning of the Augsburg Confession as it was originally submitted."[39] The Augsburg Confession is referred to as a "Christian Confession," and considered "a genuinely Christian symbol which all true Christians ought to accept next to the Word of God."[40] Those who departed from its teaching were not merely considered un-Lutheran; they were thought to have departed from the Christian faith. The Formula of Concord was written in order to preserve the truth and unity of the church, not to safeguard the dubious integrity of a sect.

The constitution, Chapter 2, identifies the ELCA with this vision of greater wholeness of Christ's people. First of all, it confesses the Triune God—Father, Son, and Holy Spirit. The gospel is identified as the "power of God for the salvation of all who believe." "God fashions a new creation" through the life, death, and resurrection of Christ. The ELCA also "confesses the Gospel, recorded in the Holy Scriptures and confessed in the ecumenical creeds and Lutheran confessional writings, as the power of God to create and sustain the church for God's mission in the world." The constitution also affirms that "the church exists both as an inclusive fellowship and as local congregations gathered for worship and Christian service. Congregations find their fulfillment in the universal community of the Church, and the universal Church exists in and through congregations."

The "Statement of Purpose" of the ELCA constitution declares that the commitment of the church is both to Lutheran unity and to Christian unity. The church shall "seek unity in faith and life with all Lutherans within its boundaries and be ready to enter union negotiations whenever such unity is manifest" (4.03.d.). The ELCA shall also "develop relationships with communities of other faiths for dialog and common action" (4.03.f.).

The understanding of ecumenism of the ELCA embraces more than Lutheran denominations. The ELCA gives God thankful praise for the movement toward agreement with other churches.

## NOTES

1. See Epitome I, 3. in the Formula of Concord, Theodore G. Tappert, ed., *The Book of Concord: The Confessions of the Evangelical Lutheran Church* (Philadelphia: Fortress Press, 1959), 465.

2. See Leif Grane, *The Augsburg Confession: A Commentary* (Minneapolis: Augsburg, 1987), 18: "The AC does not intend to initiate anything. It does not intend to create any new church doctrine. Rather, its purpose is simply to reproduce what is taught in the Christian church. Its entire design is alien to any sense of what we have come to understand as confessionalism."

See also Eric W. Gritsch and Robert W. Jenson, *Lutheranism: The Theological Movement and Its Confessional Writings* (Philadelphia: Fortress Press, 1976), vii. The Lutheran confessions are defined as "authoritative documents of a theological movement within the church catholic." The confessions are "proposals of dogma"(5). "Lutheranism is a *confessional movement* within the church catholic that continues to offer to the

whole church that proposal of dogma which received definitive documentary form in the Augsburg Confession and the other writings collected in *The Book of Concord*.
. . . The Lutheran confessions are not primarily the constitution of an established denomination or territorial church; they are rather the manifesto of a movement whose ecumenical hour – if it has one – is still partly in the future"(6).

3. The Augsburg Confession, Conclusion 5. (The Augsburg Confession is hereafter referred to as CA unless it is quoted material. Occasionally AC will be used.)

4. CA, Preface, 13.

5. Gritsch and Jenson, *Lutheranism*, 6. Cf. Grane, *The Augsburg Confession*, 68, with regard to the Augsburg Confession: "In a sense, it could be claimed that the entire AC is about this one article alone, justification by faith."

6. Gritsch and Jenson, *Lutheranism*, 42.

7. Epitome I, 1.

8. CA VII, 1.

9. Large Catechism II in *The Book of Concord*, ed. Theodore G. Tappert (Philadelphia: Fortress Press, 1959), 56.

10. Large Catechism II, 51.

11. Epitome I, 2.

12. Apology to the Augsburg Confession XXIV, 95.

13. CA, Summary of the articles on faith and doctrine, 1; Apology IV, 389. See the reference to patristic quotations in *Die Bekenntnisschriften*, 6., durchgesehene Auflage (Göttingen: Vandenhoeck & Ruprecht, 1967), 1145-55.

14. See Peter Frankel, *Testimonia Patrium* (Geneva: E. Droz, 1961).

15. Treatise on the Power and Primacy of the Pope, 39.

16. Smalcald Articles, appendix to Melanchthon's signature.

17. Quoted in Heiko Augustinus Oberman's, *Luther: Man Between God and the Devil*, trans. Eileen Wallaser-Schwarzbart (New Haven, CT: Yale University Press, 1989), 237.

18. See James E. Andrews and Joseph A. Burgess, eds., *Invitation to Action* (Philadelphia: Fortress Press, 1984), 66.

19. Epitome XII, 2.

20. CA, Conclusion, 5.

21. CA, Conclusion to Part I, 2.

22. CA, Conclusion to Part I, 1.

23. Large Catechism II, 47-53.

24. CA XXVIII, 71-72.

25. CA XXVIII, 77.

26. For ceremonies see Gritsch and Jenson, *Lutheranism*, 173: "The term 'ceremonies' should be taken as widely as possible. The provision asserts the historically of the gospel: that the liturgical, hierarchical, legal, and dogmatic arrangements for the preaching of the gospel and performing of its sacraments are the responsibility of free human creativity, and that therefore they will legitimately vary from time to time and place to place. . . . In the Lutheran view, if Christians have mutual recognition and acceptance of 'preaching' and mutual recognition of and acceptance at the eucharistic table, we thereby achieve all that must necessarily be achieved be-

tween us. For a Lutheran understanding, *communion in sacris* . . . is the main ecumenical goal, and is not necessarily the beginning of any further organizational or legal unification.

"The essential unity of the church, for Lutheranism, is neither an inward and invisible 'spiritual' unity nor an institutional unity, but unity in proclamation and sacramental action. This unity is necessary for the church; and where it is lost, we must work to recover it. The work involved will ordinarily be institutional work, and will create various organizational unities; but these latter are by-products."

27. See Gritsch and Jenson, *Lutheranism*, 173-74: "our situation is one of lost unity; we turn to the Lutheran confessions above all for help in the work of achieving renewed unity." There is, moreover, a "hermeneutical gap" between the confessions and our situation, for the confessions know nothing of modern denominationalism. CA assumes that "insofar as churchly plurality interferes with communion in holy things, this interference should be overcome – unless, of course, it should develop that one party had ceased altogether to be the church." What is demanded is not a demand for dogmatic unity, the actual preaching of the gospel. "Nor does 'it is sufficient' single out some set of essential doctrines on which there must be agreement."

28. The newly adopted Constitution of the Lutheran World Federation (VIII Assembly, Curitiba, February 1990) and the "Message" of the Assembly (Part I) represent a contemporary Lutheran affirmation of the relationships between confessional unity and *communio in sacris*.

29. George Wolfgang Forell and James F. McCue, eds., *Confessing One Faith: A Joint Commentary on the Augsburg Confession by Lutheran and Catholic Theologians* (Minneapolis: Augsburg, 1982), 175.

30. Formula of Concord, Solid Declaration X, *The Book of Concord: The Confessions of the Evangelical Lutheran Church*, ed. Theodore G. Tappert (Philadelphia: Fortress Press, 1959), 5. (Hereafter the Solid Declaration is referred to as SD.)

31. SD, Summary Formulation, 1.

32. See Eugene L. Brand, *Towards a Lutheran Communion: Pulpit and Altar Fellowship*, LWF Report no. 26 (Geneva: Lutheran World Federation, 1988), 86: "Lutherans must admit that CA7 has often been applied out of context in grossly minimalistic and anti-structural ways. But when it is understood as spoken from within the ecclesial communion to uphold the gospel through which Christ (source and focus of communion) is present in the Holy Spirit among his people, it can help determine wherein the consensus implicit in confessional communion consists and where there is room for theological diversity."

33. Small Catechism II in *The Book of Concord*, 6.

34. Epitome I, 5.

35. Small Catechism, Preface, 24.

36. SD, Introduction, 6.

37. SD, Introduction, 9.

38. SD, Summary Formulation, 11.

39. SD, Antitheses in the Controverted Articles, 20.

40. SD, Introduction, 4.

# 3
# Ecumenical Heritage

The twentieth century has brought continuous, active, and official involvement of churches, including predecessors of the Evangelical Lutheran Church in America, in the quest to overcome Christian division and, by God's Spirit, to express the visible unity of Christ's people. The ecumenical movement needs to be seen as the stirring of Christians under the Spirit's prompting to disclose to those around them God's call for the church to be one. This movement is, therefore, much more than conferences and meetings of councils of churches, although such events serve as landmarks for the ecumenical movement.

Prior to World War II, Lutherans from the churches of northern Europe and some from North America were present at World Missionary Conferences, a major impetus to the modern ecumenical movement, as well as Faith and Order Conferences and Life and Work Conferences. It is true that American Lutherans were initially hesitant and cautious, with some remaining more guarded, because of their concern for confessional truth, while others with the same concern for confessional truth were becoming more open to ecumenical participation. The conferences eventually became part of a more continuous and unified organization, the World Council of Churches.

## Councils of Churches
By 1948, North American Lutherans took a prominent place in the formation of the World Council of Churches and successfully insisted that the representation from churches be determined in a major way according to confessional families. Within a decade, almost all of the ante-

cedents to the Evangelical Lutheran Church in America held membership in the council. At that time Lutherans made up the largest confessional group in the council. The council has given significant attention to issues of Christian unity, mission, and service.

In varying degrees the uniting churches and their members have participated in state and local councils of churches, and in the National Council of the Churches of Christ in the U.S.A. Such involvement brought greater understanding of the opportunities and challenges of ecumenical activity.

## Ecumenical Dialogues

By 1950, many North American Lutherans were fully committed to ecumenical partnership around the world and in this country. In the next decade, they were involved actively in the development of ecumenical dialogues. After 1965, these dialogues received new stimulus from the entry of the Roman Catholic Church into the ecumenical movement, an event marked and ratified by the Second Vatican Council. Other dialogues were continued or initiated with Reformed and Presbyterians, Episcopalians, United Methodists, Orthodox, Baptists, and conservative evangelicals. Participation in the dialogues by the predecessor bodies of the Evangelical Lutheran Church in America was unified through the National Lutheran Council, later the Lutheran Council in the U.S.A., and the Lutheran World Federation. Lutheran unity and Christian unity were progressing together.

By 1982, when official approval was given for a commission to plan the union that produced the Evangelical Lutheran Church in America, ecumenical developments were expanding rapidly.

## Lutheran World Federation

The membership and active role of the uniting churches in the Lutheran World Federation produced new ecumenical perceptions. At the assembly in 1984, the member churches of the federation declared themselves to be in *altar and pulpit fellowship*. This declaration may have profound effects on the nature of the federation itself and on the churches' understandings of their relationships to one another and to nonmember churches. That assembly also adopted the following understanding of unity, which is compatible with the vision set forth in the accompanying document statement of the Evangelical Lutheran Church in America:

> The true unity of the church, which is the unity of the body of Christ and participates in the unity of the Father, Son, and Holy Spirit, is given in and through proclamation of the Gospel in Word and Sacrament. This unity is expressed as a communion in the common and at the same time, multiform

confession of one and the same apostolic faith. It is a communion in Holy Baptism and in the eucharistic meal, a communion in which the ministries exercised are recognized by all as expressions of the ministry instituted by Christ in his church. It is a communion where diversities contribute to fullness and are no longer barriers to unity. It is a committed fellowship, able to make common decisions and to act in common.

The diversity present in this communion rises out of the differing cultural and ethnic contexts in which the one church of Christ lives out its mission and out of the number of church traditions in which the apostolic faith has been maintained, transmitted, and lived throughout the centuries. In recognizing these diversities as expressions of the one apostolic faith and the one catholic church, traditions are changed, antagonisms overcome, and mutual condemnations lifted. The diversities are reconciled and transformed into a legitimate and indispensable multiformity within the one body of Christ.

This communion lives out its unity in confessing the one apostolic faith. It assembles in worship and in intercession for all people. It is active in common witness to Jesus Christ; in advocacy for the weak, poor, and oppressed; and in striving for peace, justice, and freedom. It is ordered in all its components in conciliar structures and actions. It is in need of constant renewal and is at the same time, a foretaste of that communion, which the Lord will at the end of time bring about in his kingdom.

**American Lutherans were encouraged by the ecumenical participation in the celebration of the 450th anniversary of the Augsburg Confession in 1980 and the 500th anniversary of the birth of Martin Luther in 1983.**

For eight decades Lutherans have been involved in work geared to achieving a greater degree of cooperation among Christian churches and a more complete manifestation of Christian unity. Since the modern ecumenical movement took structural form in the 1920s, Lutherans have been challenged to examine their relations with other Christian communions and to look carefully at the theological rationale for their own separate existence.[1] They have been deeply involved in what may prove to be the most urgent theological task of the twentieth century—reflection on the nature of the church.

## COUNCILS OF CHURCHES

Lutherans were leaders of, and active participants in, the universal Christian conference on Life and Work and the world conference on Faith and Order prior to the formation of the World Council of Churches (WCC).

For example, Archbishop Nathan Söderblom of the Church of Sweden was the host of the first Life and Work conference in 1925. Statements made by Lutherans on the issue of church relationships in that meeting mark the beginning of Lutherans' ongoing efforts to clarify and contribute to the ecumenical debate on ecclesiastical relationships.

In the conferences of 1925 (Life and Work) and 1927 (Faith and Order), Lutherans asserted that the sort of spiritual compulsion that forces similarity through authority, or by commanding uniformity, was a dangerous enemy to Christian unity.[2] Lutherans insisted upon the recognition of the confessional principle in any design for Christian unity. These early utterances demonstrate that Lutherans, as other Christians in large numbers around the world, had been touched by the call to common Christian endeavors. Strong impulses to ecumenical action were seen in the gospel and in Luther. With the conviction that there is no conflict between confessionality and ecumenicity, Lutherans engaged in the preparatory work that lay behind the formation of the Lutheran World Federation (1947), the World Council of Churches (1948), and regional organizations like the National Council of the Churches of Christ in the U.S.A. (1950).

Lutherans struggled to gain acceptance of the confessional principle as a guide for Lutheran ecumenical relations in the decade preceding the birth of the WCC.[3] Thinking among the committees working on the formation of the World Council tended towards territorialism. The Executive Committee of the Lutheran World Convention in 1938 asserted that representation in the proposed WCC Assembly, Central Committee, and committees be "ecclesiastical and confessional and not territorial."[4] First they argued that confessional communities should be permitted to compare views among themselves within the program work of the WCC. They saw sectionalism to be a much greater danger than sectarianism. Secondly, the Lutheran World Convention leadership was convinced that the WCC must be constituted by the churches accepting membership. They envisaged the unhappy prospect of an ecumenical movement operating above and outside the churches. As a result of these Lutheran initiatives, the First Assembly of the WCC in Amsterdam voted unanimously for the following constitutional amendment:

> Seats in the Assembly shall be allocated to the member churches by the Central Committee, due regard being given to such factors as numerical size, adequate confessional representation and adequate geographical distribution.[5]

The Lutheran petition was granted, at least in principle; in practice it has proved difficult to implement.

Since 1948, Lutherans from around the world have been energetically involved in working within the WCC as the organization carries out its five central tasks. These tasks are (1) to call the churches to the goal of visible unity in one faith and eucharistic fellowship; (2) to facilitate the common witness of the churches in each place and in all places; (3) to support their efforts at common witness and evangelism; (4) to express their concern for the service of human need and the promotion of justice and peace; and (5) to foster the renewal of the churches in unity, worship, mission, and service.

The National Council of the Churches of Christ in the U.S.A. (NCCC) came into existence in December 1950. Many of the twenty denominations that approved the establishment of the organization were Lutheran. At the time of its formation in 1988, the ELCA voted to be a member of the NCCC, and reaffirmed that commitment in 1989, continuing the long-standing Lutheran membership in this conciliar organization.

The NCCC is constituted by churches, not individuals; its purpose is to provide a place for member denominations to work together. In 1981, the preamble to the constitution was amended to say that the NCCC is a "community of communions." Member churches of the council continue to define and give structural expression to what the concept of "community of communions" means for their life together. Throughout its history, the organization has spoken to and with its members, not for them; the NCCC is not a superchurch. Article V, Section 2 of the constitution states:

> The Council shall have no authority or administrative control over the churches which constitute its membership. It shall have no authority to prescribe a common creed, form a church government, or form of worship, or to limit the autonomy of the churches cooperating with it.

Through the NCCC, Lutherans have been able: (1) to manifest more completely the oneness of the church; (2) to encourage the use of the Bible; (3) to carry on programs of renewal in the life of the churches; (4) to extend works of Christian service throughout the world; (5) to speak on moral and ethical issues facing Christians and people of other faiths; and (6) to encourage cooperation among churches and agencies at the local and regional levels.

## ECUMENICAL DIALOGUES

For more than two decades Lutherans have been involved in dialogue locally, regionally, and worldwide with a variety of partners. On the international level, the Lutheran World Federation (LWF), through its offices in Geneva, functions as a counterpart to the Secretariat for Promoting Christian Unity (Rome) [now known as the Pontifical Council], the Anglican Consultative Council (London), the World Alliance of Reformed Churches (Geneva), and to other such Christian world communions. In the United States, the Lutheran Council in the U.S.A. (LCUSA) and the U.S.A. National Committee of the LWF staffed the dialogues until the formation of the ELCA in 1988.

Lutherans have linked national and international dialogues in a number of ways.[6] The purpose of relating the two efforts is to coordinate work and avoid duplication. Impetus to progress in the dialogues sometimes comes at the national or regional level, sometimes at the world level. For example, the Leuenberg Agreement of 1973 among Lutheran, Reformed, Union, and other related churches in Europe has had influence in Latin America and the United States. The recent publication entitled *The Leuenberg Agreement and Lutheran-Reformed Relationships*[7] reflects an effort to evaluate the importance of the Leuenberg Agreement for the North American situation. The Lutheran-Reformed Committee for Theological Conversations involving the ELCA, the United Church of Christ, the Reformed Church in America, and the Presbyterian Church in the U.S.A. has been working since 1988. It builds upon international developments in Lutheran-Reformed relations, and particularly upon the previous U.S.A. dialogues (1963-66); (1972-74); and (1981-83).[8]

The results of the Lutheran-Episcopal dialogue (1982) coupled with the Anglican-Lutheran International Conversations (1970-72) contributed to the Report of the Anglican-Lutheran European Regional Commission (1982) as it recommended "provision for fuller mutual participation in Eucharistic worship." In 1983 the Joint Working Group at Cold Ash (Great Britain)[9] urged "interim Eucharist hospitality," with "steps towards fuller communion." The current discussions at the world and the U.S.A. levels on ministry and *episcopé* build upon these earlier developments in Anglican-Lutheran relations, most importantly upon the 1982 Lutheran-Episcopal Agreement in the U.S.A. that includes "Interim Sharing of the Eucharist."[10]

Regional dialogue between Methodists and Lutherans was stimulated by the results of the international Lutheran-Methodist Joint Commission that met between 1979 and 1984.[11] The world-level report entitled *The Church: Community of Grace* recommended "full fellowship of word and sacrament." The Vereinigte Evangelisch-Lutherische Kirche Deutschlands (VELKD) approved altar and pulpit fellowship with the Methodists in Germany in 1986. The statement released by the ELCA and United Methodist dialogue commission in November of 1988 entitled *Episcopacy: A Lutheran/United Methodist Common Statement to the Church*[12] builds on the work done in other regions of the world and at the global level between the LWF and the World Methodist Council.

Work of the international Lutheran-Orthodox dialogue began in 1981, and is closely related to regional dialogues in Europe and elsewhere; some dating back to the 1950s. In turn, the result of the second round of the Lutheran-Orthodox dialogue in the U.S.A., *Christ in Us, Christ for Us,* on salvation and *theosis,* will make an important contribution to other regional efforts as well to the world-level dialogue.[13]

The U.S.A.-based Baptist-Lutheran dialogue, which took place between 1979 and 1981,[14] was paralleled by conversations between German Baptists and the VELKD representatives; these efforts led to a series of international meetings beginning in 1986. The removal of sixteenth-century condemnations of the Anabaptists and the Baptist recognition of the validity of infant baptism have been under discussion.

Documentary results of international and U.S.A. Lutheran-Roman Catholic dialogue are extensive. In world-level Lutheran-Roman Catholic dialogue, following the 1971 "Malta Report," a newly formed commission (LWF/SPCU) worked on the Lord's Supper, ministry and ecclesiology.[15] In February of 1990 the U.S.A. dialogue commission completed its eighth round of dialogue on "The One Mediator, the Saints, and Mary." This has been preceded by rounds of dialogue that produced seven other volumes of results on the following topics: Justification, Teaching Authority and Infallibility in the Church, Papal Primacy, Eucharist and Ministry, the Eucharist as Sacrifice, Baptism, and the Nicene Creed.[16]

Past and current developments in our Lutheran bilateral relations are difficult to separate from recent trends in the ecumenical movement. One dramatic trend that has emerged in the last two decades is the convergence of thinking among world Christians on matters of basic Christian doctrine. An important example is the *Baptism, Eucharist and Ministry* (BEM) text produced in 1982 by the Faith and Order Commission of the World Council of Churches. The convergence in Christian thinking reflected in this text has been partly responsible for the new level of ecumenical commitment on the part of many communions or churches around the world. Lutheran theologians made important contributions to this multilateral dialogue process that dates back five decades. Official Lutheran responses to the BEM text have greatly enriched the discussion of these basic ecumenical issues among member churches of the WCC.[17]

## LUTHERAN WORLD FEDERATION

In a review of the LWF's work between the Seventh World Assembly in Budapest (1984) and the Eighth World Assembly in Curitiba (1990), the

General Secretary of the Lutheran World Federation says one theme from Budapest has become the key that offers access to all the others present in the life of the LWF. He goes on to make the following comments:

> That is the theme of communion (*koinonia*), set forth in the *Statement on the Self-Understanding and Task of the LWF*. Communion is not a new theme for Lutherans. Its emergence at Budapest is the result of a lengthy development which antedates the LWF itself.
>
> As key, communion unlocks the entire spectrum of our work which has been theological and churchly, not in any restrictive sense but in the consciousness that we are a people participating in God's mission to and for the World. Our work demonstrates that acting out of a clear confessional basis leads to engagement in all facets of the world God made and has redeemed.[18]

As this quotation indicates, the interrelationship among confessionality, ecclesiology, and ecumenicity in the life and thought of Lutherans has nowhere been more evident than in the work of the LWF. Basic to the deliberations dating back to the 1920s, which took place in LWF predecessor organizations, was a concern for confessionality.[19]

Generally, confession has been seen by Lutherans to be neither exclusive nor divisive. When the confessions were formulated, the term *concordia* was used to describe that by which the unifying impulses in the church were to find clearer expression. Confession is seen as an event in the life of the church; it shapes its proclamation and helps to focus that proclamation upon the central message of the Bible. In 1977, at the LWF Assembly in Dar es Salaam, the Federation declared that the political policy of *apartheid* of the government of South Africa, which prohibits Christian sisters and brothers from joining in worship because of race, is an issue *status confessionis* – it violates the Lutheran understanding of the church as expressed in CA VII. This action pointed to the fundamental commitment to Christian unity to which the confessions bind Lutherans. The history of the LWF documents how confessionality is appropriated by member churches in their ongoing interaction with the challenges of the times.

What comprises Lutheran confessionality is a question that has been long debated, most intensively at the Helsinki Assembly in 1963. The various elements of Lutheran confessionality that have been affirmed on different occasions were listed in a paper presented by Professor Harding Meyer to the LWF Executive Committee in 1972. The list reads as follows:

> 1. Understanding of salvation in terms of justification of the sinner by faith through the grace of God in Jesus Christ;
> 2. Emphasis on the divine *kenosis* or condescension, and on the principle of *finitum capax infiniti*, [the finite is capable of the infinite] which is decisive both for christology and for an understanding of word and sacrament;

3. Concern for a clear distinction between law and gospel with its soteriological as well as ethical and socio-ethical implications;

4. Understanding of Holy Scripture characterized by the distinction between gospel and Scripture, between *viva vox evangelii* [living voice of the Gospel] and the written word of the Bible;

5. Emphasis on proclamation of the gospel and administration of the sacrament as the constitutive elements of the church, and, consequently, insistence upon freedom with regard to forms and manifestations of church order, church structure, and church life;

6. Persistent theological and critical quest for the truth of the gospel to be proclaimed here and now;

7. Insistence upon church confessions.[20]

Through the years the debates on confessionality, ecclesiology, and ecumenicity in the LWF have often pointed to the danger that Lutheran confessionality may become Lutheran confessionalism, which puts a confessional interpretive system in place of the Bible, the historic creeds, and the sixteenth-century Lutheran Confessions. Of course the danger of confessionalism also exists among those who are content with a lack of formulated confessions, or among those for whom ecumenism of some kind takes the shape of doctrinaire "ideology."

In the last decade a dramatic development in relationship to confessionality has occurred in the life of world Lutheranism. A clear convergence of thinking, if not a consensus of thought on the *communio* character of Lutheranism, is now emerging.[21] Some Lutherans have spoken of pulpit and altar fellowship as the way Lutherans understand communion. Others have affirmed a different way of understanding confessional communion, which is basic to ecclesial communion and *communio in sacris*. Throughout the years, and particularly the last decade, the argument within the LWF has been an ecclesiological one rather than one accenting the correct doctrine(s) by which the church is to be understood. This argument seriously considers the intention of the Augsburg Confession and its Apology to confess the orthodox, catholic faith.

In his survey of LWF reflection and action on the question of the *communio*, Eugene Brand writes the following:

> While it is true that CA7 constitutes a break with the medieval concept of the church as grace-dispensing institution, that break is made precisely in the interest of restoring a biblical, patristic communio ecclesiology. Concentration on the *satis est* should not overshadow the point of departure in CA7: "(ein heilige christliche Kirche) ist die Versammlung aller Gläubigen . . ." (One holy Christian church) is the assembly of all believers . . . The church is not individuals, the church is a "*gathering* (assembly) of people" – "not the persons

simply as such, but something that happens with them, as the concrete occurrence of their reality as community." [Gritsch and Jenson, *Lutheranism*, 130.] That this gathering or assembly is to be understood as *koinonia*, as participation in Christ, is clear from the rest of CA7 which speaks about what happens within the gathering: the gospel is preached "in conformity with a pure understanding of it" and the sacraments are administered "in accordance with the divine word." [*Book of Concord*, 32.]

If one reads this article in the context of the explicit intention of the confession, it will be seen to specify what happens in the gatherings called church. It does not purport to identify church with bodies having a correct theological position in preaching and sacraments. [Gritsch and Jenson, *Lutheranism*, 132f.] The gospel event is what is central to and constitutive of the church, not theological correctness or historical structures. Thus a Lutheran approach to communio places a heavy emphasis on confessional communion. Where confessional communion is understood ecclesiologically, i.e., where it is inextricably bound with ecclesial communion and *communio in sacris*, it can be an ecumenical contribution as well as provide the key to an adequate Lutheran self-understanding. But where confessional communion is understood in terms of correct theology, it is destructive of ecclesial communion both confessionally and ecumenically.[22]

The emergence of this ecclesiological view of *communio* within world Lutheranism might prompt some to say that Lutherans are limiting the concept of communion in a sectarian fashion. Brand asserts the opposite in the survey just quoted. He notes that the Lutheran communion is a vital participant in the total *communio sanctorum*. He recalls that in the Large Catechism, Luther makes the connection between communion and unity and, in his 1519 treatise on the Eucharist, links sacramental communion with ecclesial communion.[23] Lutheran emphasis upon confessional communion does not imply that it is exclusively Lutheran.[24]

The LWF has taken the position that the presently existing confessional communion is sufficient for ecclesial communion and that *communio in sacris* must follow. Many theological dialogues have cited and described degrees of ecclesial communion and affirmed that the goal of full communion is achieved through a process. This is an affirmation borne out by the experience of Lutherans worldwide as they reflect on their ecumenical heritage.

## NOTES

1. See Daniel F. Martensen, *The Federation and the World Council of Churches*, LWF Report no. 3 (Geneva: Lutheran World Federation, 1978), 1-9.

2. Note Abdel Ross Wentz, "Lutheran Churches and the Modern Ecumenical

Movement," *World Lutheranism of Today: A Tribute to Anders Nygren* (Stockholm: Svenska Kyrkans Diakonistyrelses Bokforlag, 1950), 394-95.

3. For a discussion of the debate see Giovanni Cireti, *Ecumenismo corso di Metodologica ecumenica* (Rome: Instituto di Teologia, 1986).

4. Wentz, *World*, 407. See Harold E. Fey, ed., *A History of the Ecumenical Movement*, vol. 2 (Philadelphia: Westminster Press, 1970). See also the discussion in E. Clifford Nelson, *The Rise of World Lutheranism: An American Perspective* (Philadelphia: Fortress Press, 1982) and Dorris A. Flesner, *American Lutherans Help Shape World Council: The Role of the Lutheran Churches of America in the Formation of the World Council of Churches,* Lutheran Historical Conference Publication no. 2 (Dubuque, IA: Wm. C. Brown Company, 1981).

5. *Amsterdam: August 22-September 4, 1948,* ed. W.A. Visser't Hooft (London: SCM Press, 1949), 198-99.

6. Harding Meyer and Lukas Fisher, eds., *Growth in Agreement,* Faith and Order Paper no. 108 (New York: Paulist Press; Geneva: World Council of Churches, 1984). See also Günther Gassmann and Nils Ehrenström, *Confessions in Dialogue: A Survey of Bilateral Conversations Among World Confessional Families 1962-1971,* Faith and Order Paper no. 63 (Geneva: World Council of Churches, 1972).

7. William G. Rusch and Daniel F. Martensen, eds., *The Leuenberg Agreement and Lutheran-Reformed Relationships* (Minneapolis: Augsburg, 1990).

8. Paul C. Empie and James I. McCord, eds., *Marburg Revisited: A Reexamination of Lutheran and Reformed Traditions* (Minneapolis: Augsburg, 1966) and James E. Andrews and Joseph A. Burgess, eds., *An Invitation to Action: Dialogue Series III, 1981-1983* (Philadelphia: Fortress Press, 1984). These two books were a result of these dialogues. See also *Toward Church Fellowship* (Geneva: Lutheran World Federation and the World Alliance of Reformed Churches, 1989).

9. See *Anglican-Lutheran Relations,* Report of the Anglican-Lutheran Joint Working Group (London: Anglican Consultative Council; Geneva: Lutheran World Federation, 1983).

10. See *The Niagara Report: Report of the Anglican-Lutheran Consultation on Episcope*, published for the Anglican Consultative Council and the Lutheran World Federation (London: Church House Publishing, 1988).

11. See *The Church: Community of Grace*, Lutheran-Methodist Dialogue, 1979-1984 (Lake Junaluska, NC: World Methodist Council; Geneva: Lutheran World Federation, 1984).

12. Copies are available from the Office for Ecumenical Affairs of the ELCA, Chicago.

13. Robert Tobias and John Meyendorff, eds., *Salvation in Christ: A Lutheran-Orthodox Dialogue* (Minneapolis: Augsburg, forthcoming).

14. See the volume of the *American Baptist Quarterly* entitled "Lutheran-Baptist Dialogues," 1.2 (December 1982).

15. These and other texts are published in *Growth and Agreement.* See note 6.

16. These volumes, published by Augsburg, are available from Augsburg Fortress, Publishers, Minneapolis.

17. See Max Thurian, *Churches Respond to BEM*, 6 vols. (Geneva: World Council of Churches, 1986-88).

18. *From Budapest to Curitiba*, LWF Report no. 27 (Geneva: Lutheran World Federation, 1989), 7. See also the official *Report of the Eighth Assembly*, Lutheran World Federation, Curitiba, Brazil, 1990, especially Part I of the "Message" (Geneva: Lutheran World Federation, 1990) and the new LWF constitution on which positive action was taken at Curitiba. See also *Communio/Koinonia*, A Study by the Institute for Ecumenical Research (Geneva: Institute for Ecumenical Research, 1990), included in this volume as Appendix 2.

19. See *Lutheran Identity* (Strasbourg: Institute for Ecumenical Research, 1977) and the multivolume document entitled *The Identity of the Church and Its Service to the Whole Human Being* (Geneva: Lutheran World Federation Department of Studies, 1977).

20. Harding Meyer, "The LWF and Its Role in the Ecumenical Movement," *Lutheran World*, 20.1 (1973): 19. See also *Lutheran Identity*.

21. See "Message" in *Report of Eighth Assembly*, Lutheran World Federation, Curitiba, Brazil, 1990 (Geneva: Lutheran World Federation, 1990).

22. Eugene L. Brand, *Toward a Lutheran Communion: Pulpit and Altar Fellowship*, LWF Report no. 26 (Geneva: Lutheran World Federation, 1988), 77-78.

23. Brand, *Toward*, 82-83.

24. Walter Kasper, "The Church as Communion," *Theology & Church* (London: SCM Press, 1989), 148-65. See also John D. Zizioulas, *Being as Communion* (Crestwood, NY: St. Vladamir's Press, 1985).

# 4
## Lutheran Unity

*Positions of the Uniting Churches*
In 1978, The American Lutheran Church and the Lutheran Church in America approved "A Statement on Communion Practices." Section II, Recommendations for Practice, adopted by both churches in convention, included a subsection on intercommunion. This sub-section provided guidance for eucharistic sharing in Lutheran settings and ecumenical gatherings.

At its eleventh biennial convention in 1982, the Lutheran Church in America approved as its official position the document, *Ecumenism: A Lutheran Commitment.* This statement became a charter for a deliberate program of ecumenical study and activity. Three years later, the Church Council of The American Lutheran Church approved a similar document for that church entitled, *Ecumenical Perspective and Guidelines.* Thus two of the uniting churches had recent and strong statements expressing their rationale for ecumenical involvement.

In 1982, all three predecessor churches entered into the *Lutheran-Episcopal Agreement* with the Episcopal Church in the United States. After years of bilateral dialogues, these churches were able to enter into a new level of fellowship that provided for mutual recognition of churches, joint prayer and study, joint commitment to evangelism and mission, interim sharing of the Eucharist, future dialogue, and a commitment to work for full communion. In 1988 this agreement entered into the life of the Evangelical Lutheran Church in America.

When the third series of Lutheran-Reformed dialogues reported to the churches in 1984, its recommendations confronted the uniting churches

51

with critical questions. Acceptance of this dialogue report, *An Invitation to Action*, was uneven. All three uniting churches did recognize the Reformed Church in America and the Presbyterian Church (U.S.A.) as churches in which the Gospel is preached, and committed themselves to joint projects and at least limited common worship. The Association of Evangelical Lutheran Churches and The American Lutheran Church in 1986 entered into a new relationship with the Presbyterian Church (U.S.A.) and the Reformed Church in America. The Lutheran Church in America in 1986 took action in conformity with, but not exceeding, a *Statement on Common Practices* of 1978. With the formation of the Evangelical Lutheran Church in America, the relationships established in 1986 ended. The commitments to fuller relationships with the Reformed Church in America and Presbyterian Church (U.S.A.), made in 1986 by the three uniting churches, were left as a challenge to the Evangelical Lutheran Church in America.

All these events indicate that official reception of the results from dialogues has become a major concern as reports from the dialogues ask the sponsoring churches to take specific actions. Such requests highlight the need for the churches to take seriously the reception of the work of the dialogues into their life and faith.

### During Formation of the Evangelical Lutheran Church in America

Between 1982 and the constituting of the Evangelical Lutheran Church in America, the three bishops of the uniting churches, and other leaders, formed relationships with major church leaders throughout the world. These associations had antecedents in earlier years, but the deliberateness and intensity of the contacts in the 1980s formed new levels of trust, commitment to the unity of the church, and potential for new ecumenical advances.

In 1983, the Faith and Order Commission of the World Council of Churches transmitted to the churches for their response and reception the document, *Baptism, Eucharist and Ministry*. Two of the churches forming the Evangelical Lutheran Church in America made official responses to this text of convergences. Responses from churches around the world have demonstrated an overwhelming interest in what has become a major ecumenical process that will continue.

The years prior to the Evangelical Lutheran Church in America represent a period of rich ecumenical growth that was given to the merged church as it began its life.

## POSITIONS OF THE UNITING CHURCHES

The text of the document begins by referring to the LCA-ALC "A Statement on Communion Practices," Section II.A.7. It clearly indicates that Lutherans, who were already participating in ecumenical worship that included the Eucharist, in a clear movement away from the Galesburg Rule of 1870 ("Lutheran altars are for Lutheran communicants only"), needed both affirmation and guidance. The portion regarding ecumenical participation deserves to be quoted in full:

> Participation as a visitor in non-Lutheran congregations, *proper because of the universal nature of the church*, places one in the role of a guest. As a visitor one should respect the prevailing practice of hospitality. On such occasions and at ecumenical gatherings, in parish and non-parish settings, both pastoral and lay participation as communicants is a matter of personal judgment.
>
> Such judgment should be informed by the following considerations:
> a. The participants be baptized Christians;
> b. That the Real Presence of Christ in the Sacrament be publicly affirmed;
> c. That the Sacrament be celebrated as a Means of Grace;
> d. That the Words of Institution be proclaimed; and
> e. That the elements associated with our Lord's institution be used.
>
> For Lutheran clergy to be involved as presiding or assisting ministers in the celebration of Holy Communion in other churches, a reciprocal relationship between the congregations and clergy involved should prevail.[1]

Participation in the Eucharist on the part of many Lutherans in ecumenical settings was already acknowledged by the ALC and the LCA as it was occurring on the local level. "Intercommunion," it should be noted, as it pertains to church bodies, was not addressed in this statement. These agreements, such as the one established with the Episcopal Church in the USA in 1982, were left to be worked out, where appropriate, in the course of the various bilateral dialogues and as approved by the participating churches.

The statements on ecumenism of the LCA (*Ecumenism: A Lutheran Commitment*, 1982) and ALC (*Ecumenical Perspective and Guidelines*, 1985) each expressed a rationale for ecumenical involvement. The LCA statement defined ecumenism as "not merely a pooling of disparate gifts but proceeds from agreement in the Gospel. The Gospel is a living reality to be asserted in new situations with meaning and authority for today."[2] It further defines the partners with whom the church relates ecumenically: "Ecumenism embraces a full spectrum of churches which confess God the Father, the Son, and the Holy Spirit."[3] The statement characterizes the LCA as a "manifestation of the church evangelical, catholic, and ecumenical," drawing a distinction between "unity" (e.g., agreement in the gospel and pulpit and altar fellowship) and "union" (e.g., organizational unification). The gospel "allows for a considerable variety in many aspects of ecclesiastical life and organization, doctrinal expression, and ethical assertions." "Ecumenism calls this evangelical and catholic church to be prepared to be a bridge. . . . It does not see progress in one area as competitive with advancement in another. Each individual gain with other Christians should be welcomed by all who are ecumenically committed." Involvement in the various councils of churches is affirmed.[4] Creeds and confessions are said to "suffice for Lutheran unity," but "their authority and proven value do not preclude new formulations for new situations." Lutheran Confessions, and particularly the Augsburg Confession in its "reconciling intent," are important ecumenical resources. "Where there is agreement in the Gospel, 'eucharistic hospitality' and 'interim sharing of the eucharist' may take place and become part of the experience that moves churches toward fuller Christian unity." The evangelical and representative principles are affirmed. Bilateral and multilateral dialogues are encouraged, though this does not preclude the importance of congregational initiative. This church needs to learn from local ecumenism and offer guidance and coordination so that ecumenism in the local congregation and the ecumenical stance of this church may be in harmony.

At the conclusion of Section III, "A Review of the American Lutheran Church's Ecumenical Relations," the ALC statement called for a broad study process concerning the issues related to interchurch fellowship. It proffered a caveat that the church be mindful of the *satis est* of CA VII. "'For the true unity of the church it is enough (*satis est*) to agree concerning the teaching of the Gospel and the administration of the sacraments.' To require anything more is to fall prey to the error of separatism; to require anything less, to the error of unionism."

The statement goes on to offer guidelines beginning with the affirmation that the unity of the church is both a gift and a task. "We therefore declare our readiness to consider new forms of fellowship with other Christian churches." The 1968 guidelines governing membership in councils of churches are reiterated (the ALC voted in convention in 1970 not to apply for membership in the National Council of the Churches of Christ in the U.S.A., and after years of study, in 1982 the Church Council, likewise, voted not to pursue membership in the NCCC). These guidelines articulate the evangelical, biblical, organizational, and representational principles. The guidelines also state that "varying degrees of fellowship will be exercised as churches find their way in new circumstances and relationships." Traditional "altar and pulpit fellowship" is not the only option for establishing fellowship with other churches. It states that "no expression of fellowship . . . should be understood as a stage on the way to organizational unification. . . . Organic merger is not the immediate objective of dialog and fellowship, nor, of course, does fellowship preclude this possibility." A basic tension is said to exist between "confessional particularity, and ecumenical universality." The guidelines argue that "being confessional is proper; becoming confessionalistic and narrow impedes appropriate ecumenical involvement." They go on to observe that "being ecumenical is proper, becoming ecumenicalistic and broad impedes appropriate confessional considerations."[5] The practical suggestions conclude with an appeal to local ecumenism in language identical to that of the LCA statement.

There was a broad consensus between the two church bodies in many significant areas: a common statement of scriptural and confessional foundations; agreement on the continuing importance of the various dialogues in which Lutherans have been engaged since the early 1960s; an acknowledgment of the evangelical and representative principles; and a stress on the highly important role the local congregation plays, and must play, in ecumenism.

There are some equally significant differences: a much more cautious stance on the part of the ALC, as compared to the LCA, on the question of conciliar participation, especially with regard to the NCCC; a tendency on the part of the ALC to regard CA VII (*satis est*) in a more restrictive sense than the LCA; and an ALC rejection of the organizational unification as an ecumenical goal even if gradually achieved. Many of these questions are discussed in detail in the following chapters titled "Forms of Ecumenism" and "Goal and Stages of Relationships."

In 1982 the AELC, ALC, and LCA entered into agreement with the Episcopal Church in the USA.[6] The groundwork for this agreement was laid by three series of dialogues, one international and two on the national level. From 1969 until 1972 a U.S. Lutheran-Episcopal dialogue met under the sponsorship of the Episcopal Commission on Ecumenical Relations and the Division of Theological Studies, LCUSA (LED I). The sharing of the Lord's Supper was of special concern. The Lutheran participants agreed that the *satis est* of CA VII is satisfied when it is recognized that the gospel is actually preached and the sacraments administered so that they communicate the gospel.

The second series of dialogues met from 1976 until 1980 (LED II). Although the Lutheran Church-Missouri Synod representatives attached separate recommendations, their counterparts in the AELC, ALC, and LCA approved a statement calling, in part, for mutual recognition of church bodies and a call for interim eucharistic hospitality.

It should be noted that while full communion is not established by this agreement,[7] the Lutheran churches recognized the Episcopal Church as a community in which the gospel is preached and taught. It was agreed "that the basic teaching of each respective church is consonant with the Gospel and is sufficiently compatible with the teaching of this church that a relationship of Interim Sharing of the Eucharist is hereby established."[8] The agreement calls on Lutherans to "recognize now the Episcopal Church as a church in which the Gospel is preached and taught." The LCA commentary argues that "for Lutherans this is a maximal statement. It is always so when Lutherans speak about the preaching of the Gospel. . . . American Lutherans are stating officially for the first time that a group not subscribing to the Lutheran Confessions does fulfill the intention of those confessions." In such cases it is not necessary to agree in doctrinal statements about the gospel and the sacraments when it is recognized that the gospel is actually preached and the sacraments are actually administered in accordance with it. The Lutherans agreed to welcome Episcopalians to the table "under the Statement on Communion Practices adopted in 1978," and joint celebrations of the Eucharist were encouraged under certain guidelines.[9] The churches encouraged the development of a "common Christian life" through mutual prayer and support; common study of Scripture, history, and theological traditions; joint programs of education, theological discussion, mission, evangelism, and social action; and joint use of physical facilities.

Lutherans were not as unequivocal in their support of the third series of Lutheran-Reformed dialogues, which ended in 1984. The joint statement and study book bore the title: *An Invitation to Action: The Lutheran-Reformed Dialogue Series III, 1981-1983.*[10] Though "all three uniting churches did recognize the Reformed Church in America and the Presbyterian Church (USA) as churches in which the Gospel is preached," they did not all equally accept the results and recommendations of the dialogue. The ALC in convention voted to "enter into a new relationship" with the Reformed in 1986,[11] while the LCA, after discussion and debate, took action based on the communion practices statement of 1978.[12]

All of these issues and developments prompt the question of "reception." The various bilateral and multilateral discussions have claimed consensus and convergence in many important areas.[13] But what is next? How do the churches receive these results? Reception, which is still in the process of definition, is open to several interpretations. It is perhaps too soon to expect a final definition.[14] If reception is not easily defined in the modern ecumenical era, neither was its meaning absolutely fixed in the ancient church. William Rusch has considered the historical context of reception:

Implicit in the practice [of reception in the early church] were [sic] a view of the church as a community of local churches in fellowship with each other with gifts to share; an understanding of the faith as something to be handed down . . . an awareness that reception takes place in eucharistic communities, involves all members of the communities, and is a continuing process; and an appreciation that reception . . . is fundamental for the life of the church and Christians.[15]

Classical reception was never merely the acceptance of theological texts from church councils. It was never a merely juridical process. Rather, reception has always functioned as a continuing, ongoing process. . . . Also involved is a constant practice of interpretation and reinterpretation. Reception is not repristination, but it is the lively process of the church's drawing from the resources of its past to seize and accept the present activities of its loving Lord. It always involves one church's willingness to receive from other churches.[16]

Reception is a process whereby the church's confession is kept alive. "Reception is a rhythm within the church of receiving and re-receiving its Lord. This often entails reinterpretation and the application of that which has been received, the gospel, in new situations."[17] According to this definition of reception, a constant reinterpretation and reappropriation of the preaching of the apostles is necessary in order to safeguard its truth and to make this truth intelligible.

Rusch has outlined three component tasks of reception. "Reception in the narrow sense" is the first. "To the fullest degree consistent with integrity, the churches must own the result of the multilateral and bilateral conversations."[18] The second is "nonreception." This is a "reconsideration and rejection by the churches of those portions of their faith and life that obscure or distort the gospel as it has been understood and proclaimed through the centuries."[19] An example is the anathemas and condemnations proclaimed by the churches. The Leuenberg Agreement between Lutheran and Reformed churches calls explicitly for this to take place.[20] The third component of reception is "dereception." This aims at removing the "beliefs and practices that, though the gospel is not at stake, hinder the visible unity of the church," what Lutherans have called "adiaphora."[21]

## DURING FORMATION OF THE
## EVANGELICAL LUTHERAN CHURCH IN AMERICA

Lutherans were thrust upon the ecumenical scene as the movement toward inter-Lutheran unity advanced in North America during the late nineteenth and early twentieth centuries, and as international Lutheran cooperation was demanded, especially in the wake of the two world wars.[22] Lutherans were active, indeed instrumental, in the constitution of the NCCC and in the emergence of the World Council after World War II.[23] But the ecumenical pace quickened and discussion deepened as a result of the Second Vatican Council (1962-65). This led to the establishment of the International and North American Lutheran-Roman Catholic dialogues. In 1961 the U.S.A. National Committee of the LWF (after 1976, Lutheran World Ministries) initiated negotiations with the National Conference of Catholic Bishops about establishing a theological dialogue. The first dialogue met in 1965.[24] Other churches with whom North American Churches have been in dialogue include: Baptists, Episcopalians, Methodists, the Reformed (talks which antedated discussion with Roman Catholics), and the Orthodox.[25]

The Faith and Order Commission of the World Council of Churches transmitted the document, *Baptism, Eucharist and Ministry*, to the churches for response and reception in 1983.[26] The LCA and ALC gave official responses. We will look at each in chronological order.

The LCA response was approved at its 1984 Convention. The response underscores the distinction between reception and making a response. Reception "includes all the phases and aspects of a process by which a church makes the results of an ecumenical dialogue or statement a part of its faith and life." As "a process involving all parts of the church, all believers," it is something which "may take years and it only occurs as Christ graciously accomplishes it by his spirit."[27] A response may be seen as part of the process leading to reception. This is similar to the difference between "reception" and "recognition," which has been explained this way:

"Recognition" means basically a theological and spiritual affirmation of the other church in its special emphases, which confers on this church – as a whole or in individual elements of its belief, life or structure – legitimacy and authenticity. "Reception" means basically a theological and spiritual affirmation of the other church – as a whole or in individual elements of its belief, life or structure – which accepts and appropriates the special emphases of the other church either as its own or as contributions (in the sense of correction or complement). Therefore "recognition" and "reception" each involve a specific emphasis: "Recognition" stresses more strongly the special character of the other in its independence, and independence capable of fellowship. "Reception" emphasizes more strongly the special character of the other as containing elements to be adopted and integrated into a church's own life and thinking and into its fellowship with the other church. "Recognition" and "Reception" must go hand in hand and complement each other in efforts for church fellowship. There can be no "reception" without recognition of the legitimacy and authenticity of the other. "Recognition" calls for beginning the process of accepting and adopting the particular features of the other in as much as they represent a contribution of the life and thinking of the partner and are considered as necessary for realizing the fellowship.[28]

In offering its response to *Facing Unity*, the LCA acknowledged a common problem, namely, "how to teach authoritatively." The problem is acute for a confessional church, for "simply to repeat the words of Scripture or of the Lutheran Confessions will not suffice in the present ecumenical situation."[29] The confessions provide the momentum for exploring ecumenical commitment. The 450th anniversary of the Augsburg Confession "aided Lutherans and others to recover the ecumenical nature of the Lutheran Confessions and especially the ecumenical commitment of Article VII with its *satis est*.[30] In this context the LCA said that "we maintain in the spirit of the Augsburg Confession, especially Article VII, that questions of decision-making are open to much variation within the search for Christian unity."[31]

The Faith and Order Commission addressed four questions to the churches as it submitted to them the BEM text. Before responding to these, the LCA made some preliminary observations. If it is true that "effective steps toward the visible unity of all Christians will require a foundation in the evangelical, catholic and ecumenical tradition,"[32] the LCA asks if the evangelical part of the tradition has not been slighted at the expense of the other two. Then the LCA suggested four motifs to the Faith and Order Commission for its consideration: (1) a stronger articulation of the Word; (2) a clearer expression of the dynamic of sin and grace, stressing the sinfulness of humankind and how this condition of humanity is related to the sacraments; (3) a reconsideration of the priority of a certain period of history as normative for faith, for the gospel is the foundation of the faith in every age (*ecclesia semper reformanda est*); and (4) a wider perspective on ministry, including the active role of the universal priesthood in the proclamation of the gospel, not to be restricted to the threefold ministry, a greater stress on the pastoral sense of the ordained ministry, and a greater commitment to the ordination of women.

The LCA response reiterated that Lutherans desire to "share with the Church Catholic their understanding of the Gospel as justification by grace through faith, although they will insist neither on that vocabulary nor on that formulation in ecumenical documents."[33] BEM is also praised for reminding Lutherans of the nature of their own tradition, which is both catholic and evangelical. "In a Church Catholic, Lutherans want to say the Gospel. In a Church Evangelical they want to say a word catholic. It is in making both of these affirmations together that Lutherans are ecumenical."[34] With regard to the Eucharist, the LCA expressed appreciation for the encouragement given to the churches to celebrate and receive the Eucharist frequently, though "attention needs to be given to the rationale for frequency of communion, along with other forms of being nourished by the Word."[35]

The official ALC response was adopted at the June 1985 meeting of the Church Council. The ALC expressed concern about ambiguous language, which "reveals as much about continuing divisions among the churches as it reveals about emerging unity."[36] Since it is not clear where the document seeks to be descriptive and where it seeks to be prescriptive, this fosters confusion about the intended purpose of the text, and raises a concern about "papering over" significant differences.[37] Careful attention must also be given to "catholic" and "evangelical" concerns. It is feared that BEM reflects a conceptual framework dominated by catholic understanding, slighting evangelical understandings. "The centrality of justification by grace through faith is thereby obscured."[38] Concerns expressed by the LCA with regard to the Word, the dynamics of sin and grace and its relation to the sacraments, and the tendency to regard certain historical periods as normative are reiterated. In addition, the ALC claimed that "the text is heavily inward-directed rather then mission-oriented." There is a "subtle encouragement" to sacerdotalism and clericalism. A clearer articulation of the "servant character of the church" is needed.[39]

With regard to baptism,[40] the ALC expressed concern that BEM "does not sufficiently stress Baptism as God's own saving act."[41] It observed that "speaking of baptism itself 'as both God's gift and our human response to that gift' . . . seems to detract from the monergism of grace." With regard to the general treatment of infant baptism vs. believers' baptism, "the central issue is whether Baptism will be understood solely as God's saving activity, or whether it will be understood in terms of human response to God's saving action." To treat both equally "results in theological confusion concerning the very nature of the sacrament."

Concerning the Eucharist, objection is made to the consistent use of the word "Eucharist" as placing emphasis on human action rather than on God's action in the sacrament. Affirmation is expressed for what the document says concerning frequency of celebration; but the response expresses disappointment that forgiveness of sin was not developed as a major theme. There is a "disproportionate emphasis on the language and theology of re-presentation/anamnesis which tends to emphasize the cultic action of the community over the gift and promise of God." There is objection to describing the Lord's Supper as "the central act of the Church's worship," chiefly because of the lack of emphasis on the Word "as prior to our understanding of the sacrament." Hence, "Christ's real presence . . . is founded not on ritual act, but on the word and promise of God." Accordingly, "we are dissatisfied with the explicit emphasis of the section on the 'invocation of the Spirit,' with its particular formation of epiclesis theology." If the Spirit is what makes Christ present, then this "runs the risk of removing the mystery of Christ's presence in the sacrament as a whole and rather identifying it with a particular moment in a ritual of consecration."[42]

With regard to ministry, BEM is criticized for not adequately developing the ministry of the whole people of God as the framework within which to take up discussion of ordained ministry. "Accordingly, the roles of the laity appear neglected." A similar caution found in the LCA response is expressed with regard to the ordained reminding "the community of the divine initiative, and of the dependence of the Church on Jesus Christ"; and concerning BEM's advocacy of the threefold pattern of ministry. As did the LCA's, the response strongly supports the ordination of women. Also, while the primacy of "the ministering function" is affirmed, ministerial structure is said to be "contingent." "The church is apostolic when it carries out the functions of ministry, not necessarily when it follows traditional forms."[43]

The response concludes with a warning against "ascribing to BEM an authority greater than its status as a study document warrants." According to the responses, there was much greater caution on the part of the ALC as compared to the LCA, yet both raised similar questions and concerns related to a Lutheran understanding of the Word, sin and grace, and the relative structural freedom of the ministerial office.

## NOTES

1. Emphasis added. See *Communion Practices Study Guide*, ed. S. Anita Stauffer (Philadelphia: Fortress Press, 1980), 19: "There has been considerable theological dialogue between Lutherans and representatives of other denominations. While recognizing with great seriousness the theological differences between denominations, the ecumenical dialogues have sought to find common evangelical truth. This new openness to ecumenical relationships was reflected in the LCA's 1964 and the ALC's 1968 Communion practices statements."

2. *Ecumenism: A Lutheran Commitment* (New York: Lutheran Church in America, 1982), IV.3

3. See note 2, IV.4. Cf. *Documents of Vatican II* (Decree on Ecumenism, Introduction), 342: "Taking part in this movement, which is called ecumenical, are those who invoke the Triune God and confess Jesus as Lord and Savior."

4. *Ecumenism: A Lutheran Commitment*, IV.6: "This church acknowledges the vision of fuller unity such as has been presented by the World Council of Churches

and its Faith and Order Commission, the National Council of Churches of Christ in the U.S.A., and the Canadian Council of Churches. It affirms the value of these formulations and organizations for this stage of the ecumenical movement. Nevertheless, it realized that it may have to proceed step by step toward unity. This church also recognized that new structures for ecumenism, which do not presently exist, are possible."

5. *Ecumenical Perspective and Guidelines* (Minneapolis: The American Lutheran Church, 1985), 14.

6. For what follows, see *The Lutheran-Episcopal Agreement: Commentary and Guidelines* (New York: Division for World Mission and Ecumenism, 1983), 2-5.

7. See *Ecumenism: A Lutheran Commitment*, 6: " 'Full communion' or, more accurately expressed, 'intercommunion'—where two churches not of the same confessional family allow communicant members freely to communicate at the altar of each and where there is freedom of ministers to officiate sacramentally in either church—is not established by this agreement."

8. *Lutheran-Episcopal Agreement*, 4. The commentary states (9): "This term, 'Interim Sharing of the Eucharist,' is a new expression to describe a new relationship, based on a sufficient, not total, recognition of eucharistic teaching. Neither the Lutheran churches nor the Episcopal church are claiming a complete recognition of every point of the other's teaching about the Lord's Supper. They are stating a mutual recognition of the doctrine of the sacrament of the altar sufficient for this sharing."

9. *Lutheran-Episcopal Agreement*, 4a and 4b. Note guidelines adopted by the Executive Council of the LCA, 15-16.

10. James E. Andrews and Joseph A. Burgess, eds., *Invitation to Action* (Philadelphia: Fortress Press, 1984). See also the smaller study booklet by Michael Root and Walter Sundberg, *Study on Lutheran-Reformed Dialogue, Based on An Invitation to Action* (Minneapolis: Augsburg Publishing House, 1985). The latter was prepared by the ecumenical offices of the LCA, ALC, and AELC and contained a congregation response form.

11. *1986 Reports and Actions* of the Thirteenth General Convention of the American Lutheran Church, 1225: "Resolved, that the American Lutheran Church enter into a new relationship with Presbyterian Church in America recognizing that in these Reformed churches 'the gospel is proclaimed and the sacraments are administered according to the ordinance of Christ'; that their ordained ministries are 'valid and effective' " and that their celebrations of the Lord's Supper are "means of grace in which Christ, truly present in the sacrament, is given and received, forgiveness of sins is declared and experienced, and a foretaste of eternal life is granted" (1226). Lutheran and Reformed churches, therefore, are urged to "enter into a process of reception" (1226). See also the "Report of the General President," 498: "The ALC representatives believe the American and European dialogues have established that there is agreement between Lutherans and Calvin-oriented Reformed churches on the gospel and sacraments and that fellowship actions should result. I concur. I further believe we have no theological reason to stop now. Congregational practice throughout the church further convinces me that national church body action has

been preceded in most instances by congregational practice. If our Lutheran churches are not all at the identical point now, I believe it right that each express present positions and let the new church make its decision at the first regular convention."

12. *Minutes: Thirteenth Biennial Convention of the Lutheran Church in America,* 1986, 249. The LCA adopted a statement, which read in part: "We recognize the Presbyterian Church (USA) and the Reformed Church in America as churches in which the gospel is preached and taught and recognize their ordained ministries which announce the gospel of Christ and administer the sacraments of faith as their chief responsibility."

13. Concerning the various bilateral dialogues and the question of reception, see William G. Rusch, *Reception: An Ecumenical Opportunity* (Philadelphia: Fortress Press, 1988), 22-26. Among those in which Lutherans have been involved include dialogues with Roman Catholics, Episcopalians, Methodists, the Reformed, and the Orthodox. Each of these is at a different stage of discussion and achievement of consensus. Reception also relates to multilateral discussion, particularly with respect to the document, *Baptism, Eucharist and Ministry.* The churches are asked to prepare official responses, as the first step in a long process of reception. A response, therefore, is not to be confused with reception. See Rusch, *Reception,* 26, 67-68.

14. Rusch, *Reception,* 12.

15. Rusch, *Reception,* 43.

16. Rusch, *Reception,* 53.

17. Rusch, *Reception,* 55.

18. Rusch, *Reception,* 70.

19. Rusch, *Reception,* 71.

20. See Andrews and Burgess, *An Invitation to Action,* 70. Note also "The Procedure for Reception," 63-65.

21. Rusch, *Reception,* 71-72.

22. For the history on inter-Lutheran cooperation and Lutheran ecumenical involvement, see E. Clifford Nelson, *The Rise of World Lutheranism* (Philadelphia: Fortress Press, 1982) and E. Theodore Bachmann, *The Ecumenical Involvement of the LCA Predecessor Bodies: A Brief History, 1900-1962,* rev. 2d. ed., (New York: Division for World Mission and Ecumenism, LCA, 1982).

23. See Bachmann, *Ecumenical Involvement,* 83-101.

24. See Joseph A. Burgess and Jeffrey Gros, FSC, eds., *Building Unity: Ecumenical Dialogues with Roman Catholic Participation in the United States* (Mahwah, NJ: Paulist Press, 1989), 85-290. With regard to Lutheran-Roman Catholic relations prior to the formation of the ELCA, see also *A Correspondence Between Pope John Paul II and Bishop James R. Crumley, Jr.* (New York: Department for Ecumenical Relations, LCA, 1985). See also, *A Day of Dialogue* (New York: Department for Ecumenical Relations, 1987), which includes an address by Johnannes Cardinal Willebrands, "The Catholic Church and Ecumenical Movement," a response by Bishop James Crumley, Jr., and an exchange between U.S. Protestant and Orthodox leaders and Pope John Paul II, 11 September 1987 in Columbia, SC.

25. See *The Lutheran-Episcopal Agreement: Commentary and Guidelines* (New York:

Division for World Mission and Ecumenism, LCA, 1983); *The Niagara Report: Report of the Anglican-Lutheran Consultation on Episcope 1987* (London: Church House Publishing, 1987); see the common Lutheran-Methodist statement on baptism in the *Perkins Journal* 34 (1981); see also the most recent statement: *Episcopacy: A Lutheran/United Methodist Common Statement to the Church* (Chicago: Office for Ecumenical Affairs, ELCA, 1988); Paul Empie and James I. McCord, eds., *Marburg Revisited: A Reexamination of Lutheran and Reformed Traditions* (Minneapolis: Augsburg, 1966), James E. Andrews and Joseph A. Burgess, eds., *An Invitation to Action: The Lutheran-Reformed Dialogue Series III, 1981-1983* (Philadelphia: Fortress Press, 1984).

26. See Max Thurian, ed., *Churches Respond to BEM*, 6 vols. (Geneva: World Council of Churches, 1986-88). Also on the Catholic response: see address by Cardinal Willebrands, in *A Day of Dialogue*, 22-24.

27. *The Response of the Lutheran Church in America to Baptism, Eucharist and Ministry*, Faith and Order Paper no. 111 (New York: Department for Ecumenical Relations, Lutheran Church in America, n.d.), 3. See also 5: "Reception will not be a matter of documents, but a renewed people under the Spirit expressing their unity in Christ."

28. *Facing Unity: Models, Forms and Phases of Catholic-Lutheran Fellowship* (Geneva: Lutheran World Federation, 1989), 23-24.

29. *Response of the LCA to BEM*, 4.

30. *Response of the LCA to BEM*, 4.

31. *Response of the LCA to BEM*, 9.

32. *Response of the LCA to BEM*, 5.

33. *Response of the LCA to BEM*, 7.

34. *Response of the LCA to BEM*, 8.

35. See note 34 above.

36. *Response of the LCA to BEM*, 3.

37. *Ecumenical Perspective and Guidelines*, 3.

38. See note 37 above.

39. *Ecumenical Perspective and Guidelines*, 4.

40. See note 39 above.

41. See note 39 above.

42. *Ecumenical Perspective and Guidelines*, 5.

43. *Ecumenical Perspective and Guidelines*, 6-7.

# 5

# *The Basis: A Church That Is Evangelical, That Is Catholic, That Is Ecumenical*

The unity of the church, as it is proclaimed in the Scriptures, is a gift and goal of God. Ecumenism is the joyous experience of the unity of Christ's people and the serious task of expressing that unity visibly and structurally. Through participation in ecumenical activity, the Evangelical Lutheran Church in America seeks to be open in faith to the work of the Spirit, so as to manifest more fully oneness in Christ.

In relation to other churches, the Evangelical Lutheran Church in America, under the Lordship of Jesus Christ, understands itself and engages in God's mission as a church that is evangelical, that is catholic, and that is ecumenical.

Such a description is intended to aid this church in its ecumenical self-understanding. It is not to be seen as a replacement of the traditional marks of the church as "one, holy, catholic, and apostolic" to which this church is committed by its confessional subscription. It is not a list of characteristics required of other churches, prior to this church entering into ecumenical relations with them.

To be *evangelical* means to be committed to the Gospel of Jesus Christ (Rom. 1:16; Mark 1:1). The church is created by the Gospel. The Gospel is more than human recollection of, or our confession about, what God has done in the past, in Israel, and uniquely in Jesus of Nazareth (2 Cor. 5:19a). It is proclamation with the power of God's deed in Christ and in his resurrection (2 Cor. 5:19b-21), an event that opens to us the future of God's eternal love, who through the crucified and risen Christ justifies us, reconciles us, and makes us new creatures (2 Cor. 5:17-18). This

Gospel is unconditional in that it announces the sure and certain promise of God who in Christ justifies the ungodly by grace through faith apart from works, and without partiality intends this for all people.

To be *catholic* means to be committed to the fullness of the apostolic faith and its credal, doctrinal articulation for the entire world (Rom. 10:8b-15, 18b; Mark 13:10; Matt. 28:19-20). This word "catholic" declares that the church is a community, rooted in the Christ event, extending through all places and time. It acknowledges that God has gathered a people, and continues to do so, into a community made holy in the Gospel, which it receives and proclaims. This community, a people under Christ, shares the catholic faith in the Triune God, honors and relies upon the Holy Scriptures as authoritative source and norm of the church's proclamation, receives Holy Baptism and celebrates the Lord's Supper, includes an ordained ministry, and professes one, holy, catholic, and apostolic Church.

To be *ecumenical* means to be committed to the oneness to which God calls the world in the saving gift of Jesus Christ. It also means to recognize the brokenness of the church in history and the call of God, especially in this century, to heal this disunity of Christ's people. By the Holy Spirit, God enlivens the Church to this ministry. In claiming to be ecumenical, this church:

1. seeks to manifest the unity that God wills for the church. The future is open to God's guidance;
2. seeks to understand and value its past, its history, and its traditions in all their varied richness as gracious gifts of God, which are incomplete themselves until they finally move toward unity in Christ;
3. contributes and learns, not by attempting to reclaim the past but by moving toward the manifestation of unity in Christ and thus toward other Christians;
4. commits itself to share with others in the tasks of proclaiming the Gospel to all and of lifting up its voice and its hands to promote justice, relieve misery, and reconcile the estranged in a suffering world;
5. calls upon its members to repent of ways in which they have contributed to disunity among Christ's people by omission and commission;
6. urges each of its members to pray, both within their own church and with members of other churches, for the unity of the church, to be concerned with new attitudes, to be ready to sacrifice nonessentials, and to take action, including the reception, where possible, of ecumenical agreements, all for the unity of the church;

7. **recognizes that the burden of proof is on those who resist unity in spite of agreement in the Gospel; and**
8. **seeks to express oneness in Christ in diverse models of unity, consistent with the Gospel and mission of the church.**

The unity of the church is a gift and goal of God. This gift and goal challenges the people of God to express and live out unity structurally and visibly. This task requires openness to the Spirit as well as dedicated determination to manifest the gift of oneness in Christ more fully.

With respect to the entire body of Christ, the ELCA understands itself as a church that is evangelical, that is catholic, and that is ecumenical. Taken together, these three terms in no way suggest a replacement for the Nicene marks of the church as "one, holy, catholic, and apostolic," nor are they proposed as requirements that other churches must meet. Each term depends on the other two to bring out its full meaning and significance. The three are linked consistently throughout the document. To be ecumenical the church will also be catholic and evangelical; to be catholic it must be evangelical; and to be evangelical the church will be catholic. These three terms are always used together in complementary fashion. There is a risk that they will become mere caricatures if they are allowed to stand in isolation from each other.[1]

The use of the terms "evangelical," "catholic," and "ecumenical" does not "indicate a bias against relationships with ecclesial bodies which by their own definition are certainly 'evangelical' but may hold some animosity toward the term 'catholic,' while remaining suspicious of 'ecumenical' relationships and conciliar involvements."[2] The three terms are used together for precisely this reason. To be ecumenical means that the church is catholic, embracing the fullness of the Christian tradition throughout the ages as expressed in its various theological, ecclesiological, and liturgical traditions. To be evangelical means that the church roots any and all expressions of its life and faith in the gospel of Jesus Christ as revealed in Holy Scripture. When taken together, these terms check any significant departure from the church's ecumenical and confessional commitment.

To be "evangelical" means to be committed to the gospel of Jesus Christ (Rom. 1:16; Mark 1:11). This gospel announces to the whole world the good news that the ungodly are justified by grace through faith in Jesus Christ apart from works of law. This saving word is addressed to all people, without restriction, reservation, or prior qualification.

At the same time, every human institution and tradition is to be measured against the word of the cross. This word, without which there is no grace, salvation, or church, is the truth that is to be preserved and defended at all costs, for God's reign comes through word and faith.[3] "We cannot surrender the truth that is so clear and necessary for the church."[4] With regard to justification, "nothing in this article can be given up or compromised," for "on this article rests all that we teach and practice."[5] The word judges the church; the church stands under the word. "The word of God is and should remain the sole rule and norm of all doctrine."[6] As its final authority, the word is also the church's sure pillar and foundation. "The church is properly called 'the pillar of truth' (1 Tim. 3:15), for it retains the pure Gospel and what Paul calls the 'foundation' (1 Cor. 3:12), that is, the true knowledge of Christ and faith."[7]

The church is created by the gospel and is normed by it. The church is a creature of the word. "God provides for the public proclamation of his divine, eternal law and the wonderful counsel concerning our redemption. . . . Thereby he gathers an eternal church for himself out of the human race."[8] That the church is evangelical means that it holds unwaveringly to the center, which is Christ. Formed by the gospel and redeemed by the saving word of Christ, the church that is evangelical is not tied to any particular human tradition but is open to the call and command of God, which compels it to baptize all nations, and to recognize as brothers and sisters in the one true faith all those who confess the triune God. "We maintain that the church in the proper sense is the assembly of saints who truly believe the Gospel of Christ and who have the Holy Spirit."[9]

To be "catholic" means to be committed to the fullness of the apostolic faith and its credal, doctrinal articulation for the entire world. "We have introduced nothing, either in doctrine or in ceremonies, that is contrary to Holy Scripture or the universal church."[10] The word "catholic" declares that the church is a community, rooted in the Christ event, extending through all places and time. The creed confesses the holy catholic church "lest we take it to mean an outward government of certain nations. It is, rather, made up of men and scattered throughout the world who agree on the Gospel and have the same Christ, the same Holy Spirit, and the same sacraments, whether they have the same human traditions or not."[11] The catholic church is the universal church created and sustained by the Word, sacrament, grace, and faith. Wherever and whenever these are found, the church is present in all its fullness. The community created by the Word serves as a symbol of unity and truth. The one true faith is handed down through the tradition of the community. The confessions, building on the evangelical tradition of the church, do not address a specifically "Lutheran" body, but the apostolic church as a whole in all its catholicity. The confessions are not sectarian documents. The confessions point to the universal faith of the church, proclaimed in the Word and sacraments; they refer to the holy catholic church.

The universality of the church extends in many different directions. The catholicity of the church has great implications for its mission. As Edmund Schlink writes: "The catholicity of the church is the catholicity of its commission with which the Lord sends his people to all nations, and the catholicity of its Lord, who is present and active wherever the Gospel is preached according to his commission and the sacraments are administered."[12]

The catholic church is not a figment, an invisible ideal, but an actual community of believers. "We are not dreaming about some Platonic republic . . . but we teach that this church actually exists, made up of true believers."[13] The church, which is catholic, strives for visible unity. Structural components, while adiaphora, are not thereby considered unnecessary or unimportant.

The church, which is catholic, professes its belief in the Triune God; relies upon Scripture as authoritative source and norm of the church's proclamation; holds up the sacramental life of the church; includes an ordained ministry; and professes one, holy, catholic, and apostolic church. Catholic faith confesses the Trinity–Father, Son, and Holy Spirit–and condemns all contrary views in the church. For example, in the Solid Declaration the doctrine of the Trinity is seen as a confession of faith that unites all people called by Christ in the unity of the Spirit by the eternal will of the Father.[14]

The catholic church relies upon Scripture as the only authoritative source and norm of proclamation. "Holy Scripture remains the only judge, rule, and norm according to which as the only touchstone all doctrines should and must be understood and judged as good or evil, right or wrong."[15]

The catholic church has sacraments. While it is commonly acknowledged that the two chief sacraments of the church are Baptism and Holy Communion, the Lutherans of the sixteenth century chose not to enumerate a particular number of sacraments. Maintaining the sacramental character of the catholic church,

> We believe that we have the duty not to neglect any of the rites and ceremonies instituted in Scripture, whatever their number. We do not think it makes much difference if, for purpose of teaching, the enumeration varies, provided what is handed down in Scripture is preserved.[16]

A church that is catholic includes an ordained ministry. "If ordination is interpreted in relation to the ministry of the Word, we have no objection to calling ordination a sacrament."[17] The ministry, the purpose of which is tied to Word and faith, is instituted by God himself.[18] In addition, the office of bishop may be retained with the understanding that bishops do not exercise a temporal, but only a spiritual and pastoral authority. "Our teachers assert that according to the Gospel the power of keys or the power of bishops is a power and command of God to preach the Gospel, to forgive and retain sins, and to administer and distribute sacraments."[19]

A church that is catholic also professes one, holy, catholic, and apostolic church. These ancient marks of the church express the evangelical goal of faithfulness to the apostolic witness to the gospel of Jesus Christ and the catholic concern for visible oneness in continuity with the church's history, tradition, and mission. At Augsburg the hope was to unite the contending parties under the gospel,

> in agreement on one Christian truth, to put aside whatever may not have been rightly interpreted or treated by either side, to have all of us embrace and adhere to a single, true religion and live together in unity and in one fellowship and church, even as we are all enlisted under one Christ.[20]

To be "ecumenical" means to be committed to the oneness to which God calls the world in the saving gift of Jesus Christ. This also means that the church must recognize its brokenness and disunity, as well as the call of God, particularly as it is perceived in the ecumenical movement of the twentieth century, to heal persisting divisions. The modern conciliar movement, the challenge and continuing effects of the Second Vatican Council, the many long-standing efforts to deal seriously with matters concerning faith and order, the various bilateral and multilateral dialogues, and the progress toward greater North American and worldwide Lutheran ecclesial unity, all confront the ELCA with both challenges and opportunities to achieve the unity God wills for the church.

In claiming to be ecumenical, this church (1) seeks to manifest God's will for unity; (2) seeks to understand the church's history and traditions; (3) contributes and learns by committing itself to move forward towards unity with other Christians; (4) commits itself to proclaiming God's law and gospel, and to promote justice; (5) calls its membership into account for its own responsibility for perpetuating disunity; (6) urges its membership to pray for the unity of the church, to be prepared to sacrifice nonessentials, to take action including reception, where possible, of ecumenical agreements; (7) recognizes that the burden of proof is on those who resist unity; and (8) seeks to express oneness in Christ in diverse models, consistent with the gospel and the mission of the church.[21]

These eight proposals for specific action on the part of the ELCA seek to commit this church to the ecumenical enterprise as a practical and concrete expression of what it means to be a church that is catholic, evangelical, and ecumenical. This church professes itself to be ecumenical in this sense and towards these ends as a consequence of its catholic and evangelical heritage.

## NOTES

1. See *Ecumenism: The Vision of the Evangelical Lutheran Church in America,* "Lutheran Confessions," 4, ¶2; 5, #5; "The Stance of the ELCA," 11, ¶1-2; "Forms of Ecumenism," 12, ¶2; "Conclusion," 14.

2. *Responses to the Proposed Statement on Ecumenism of the Evangelical Lutheran Church in America* (Chicago: Office for Ecumenical Affairs, 1989), Lutheran School of Theology at Chicago Faculty Response dated 26 January 1989.

3. Large Catechism III, 53.

4. Apology of the Augsburg Confession, Preface, 16.

5. Smalcald Articles II, I, 5.

6. SD, The Summary Formulation, 9.

7. Apology of the Augsburg Confession, VII & VIII, 20.

8. SD II, 50.

9. Apology of the Augsburg Confession, VII & VIII, 28.

10. CA, Conclusion, 5.

11. Apology of the Augsburg Confession, VII & VIII, 10.

12. Edmund Schlink, *Theology of the Lutheran Confessions* (Philadelphia: Fortress Press, 1961), 208.

13. Apology of the Augsburg Confession, VII & VIII, 20.

14. SD XI, 66.

15. Formula of Concord, Epitome I, Summary, 7.

16. Apology of the Augsburg Confession XIII, 2.

17. Apology of the Augsburg Confession XIII, 11.

18. CA V, 1.

19. CA XXVIII, 5.

20. CA, Preface, 3-4.

21. See Epitome X, 7: "No church should condemn another because it has fewer or more external ceremonies not commanded by God, as long as there is mutual agreement in doctrine and in all its articles as well as in the right use of the holy sacraments."

# 6
# *The Stance of the Evangelical Lutheran Church in America*

In the constitution of the Evangelical Lutheran Church in America, Chapter 2, the Confession of Faith may be described as evangelical, catholic, and ecumenical. The Triune God, Father, Son, and Holy Spirit, is confessed, with special reference to the redeeming work of the Second Person. The canonical Scriptures are accepted as the inspired Word of God and the norm for the church's proclamation. The three ecumenical creeds are accepted as true declarations of the faith. The Augsburg Confession is accepted as a true witness to the Gospel and as a basis for unity, while the other Lutheran Confessions are accepted as valid interpretations of the faith. The language in this chapter reflects a clear and deliberate ordering of authorities, i.e., Scriptures, ecumenical creeds, confessions, in a sequence that is ancient, catholic, and ecumenical. The particularly Lutheran writings are regarded as true witnesses and valid interpretations of statements possessing higher authority. The chapter closes with a confession of the Gospel as the power of God to create and sustain the Church's mission.

These evangelical, catholic, and ecumenical characteristics of the church's confession of faith find further expression in those chapters of the constitution that deal with "Nature of the Church," (Chapter 3), "Statement of Purpose," (Chapter 4), and "Principles of Organization" (Chapter 5).

This church is bold to reach out in several directions simultaneously to all those with whom it may find agreement in the Gospel. Therefore the Evangelical Lutheran Church in America, as a member of the world-

**wide Lutheran communion, does not commit itself only to pan-Lutheranism, or to pan-Protestantism, or to Roman Catholic rapprochement or to developing relationships with the Orthodox.**

**Even more boldly, the Evangelical Lutheran Church in America takes its Lutheran theological heritage so seriously that it believes God's word of justification excludes the patterns of ecclesiastical self-justification, which have resulted from the polemical heritage of the sixteenth century. The first word, which the church speaks ecumenically, can be a word of self-criticism, a word against itself, because we are called to be seekers of a truth that is larger than all of us and that condemns our parochialism, imperialism, and self-preoccupation. If it can speak such a word of self-criticism, the church will be free to reject a triumphalistic and magisterial understanding of itself and cultivate instead an understanding of itself as a community of mission and witness that seeks to be serviceable to the in-breaking of the reign of God. In this way the ecumenical vision of the Evangelical Lutheran Church in America will not be dominated by attention to our past theological controversies and divisions. It will focus rather on *present* and *future* theological reflection and missiological action.**

The ELCA confession of faith found in Chapter 2 of its constitution may be described as evangelical, catholic, and ecumenical. These terms are mutually reinforcing. One term may not stand in isolation from the other two. The heart of this evangelical, catholic, and ecumenical faith is the doctrine of the Trinity. "This church confesses the Triune God, Father, Son, and Holy Spirit" (2.01.).

Special reference is given to the Second Person. This conforms to Luther's understanding. "The entire Gospel that we preach," he said, "depends on the proper understanding of [the second] article [of the Apostles' Creed]. Upon it all our salvation and blessedness are based."[1] The ELCA constitution states that "this church confesses Jesus Christ as Lord and Savior." He is "the Word of God incarnate, through whom everything was made and through whose life, death, and resurrection God fashions a new creation." The Word of God, which the church is charged to proclaim, begins with "the Word in creation, continuing in the history of Israel, and centering in all its fullness in the person and work of Jesus Christ." The Scriptures, as "the written Word of God," and "inspired by God's Spirit," "record and announce God's revelation centering in Jesus Christ" (2.02.).

The ELCA confesses the Triune God, as revealed in God's Word, as contained in Holy Scripture, and expressed in the ecumenical creeds of the catholic faith. "This church accepts the Apostles,' Nicene and Athanasian Creeds as true declarations of the faith of this church" (2.04.). These three chief symbols of the Christian faith are set out at the beginning of the Book of Concord, providing a catholic, evangelical, and ecumenical basis for all that follows.

The Lutheran confessional writings, based on the Word of God as revealed in Holy Scripture, and the Triune faith as professed in the ecumenical creeds, are also accepted. "This church accepts the Unaltered Augsburg Confession as a true witness to the Gospel, acknowledging as one with it in faith and doctrine all churches that likewise accept the teachings of the Unaltered Augsburg Confession" (2.05.).[2] In addition, the church accepts other writings, "namely, the Apology of the Augsburg Confession, the Smalcald Articles and the Treatise [on the Power and Primacy of the Pope], the Small Catechism, the Large Catechism, and the Formula of Concord, as further valid interpretations of the faith of the Church" (2.06.).

A clear ordering of authorities is apparent: Scripture, ecumenical creeds, confessions.[3] The same ordering is followed in the Formula of Concord. There in the Summary Formulation, Basis, Rule, and Norm, which precede the articles of the Solid Declaration, the following order is established: (1) Scripture, "the pure and clear fountain of Israel, which is the only true norm according to which all teachers and teachings are to be judged and evaluated"; (2) the three ecumenical creeds, "succinct, Christian, and based upon the Word of God"; (3) the teachings of Martin Luther, which doctrine, "drawn from and conformed to the Word of God," is summarized in the Unaltered Augsburg Confession; (4) the Apology of the Augsburg Confession; (5) the Smalcald Articles; and (6) Luther's Large and Small Catechisms, which "formulate Christian doctrine on the basis of God's Word for ordinary laymen."

Chapter 2 of the constitution closes with a confession of the gospel as the power of God to create and sustain the church's mission. "This church confesses the Gospel, recorded in the Holy Scriptures and confessed in the ecumenical creeds and Lutheran confessional writings, as the power of God to create and sustain the Church for God's mission in the World" (2.07.). Mission is described as the natural outcome of confession. Mission and confession belong together, neither to be set in isolation from the other. The church that identifies itself as a confessional body will engage in mission for the gospel's sake.

These evangelical, catholic, and ecumenical characteristics of the church's confession of faith find further expression in the chapters of the constitution that deal with the "Nature of the Church," "Statement of Purpose," and "Principles of Organization."

In the section on the nature of the church, the constitution states that "all power in the Church belongs to our Lord Jesus Christ, its head. All actions of this church are to be carried out under his rule and authority"

(3.01.). Both the church's particularity and its catholicity are acknowledged. These characteristics are not regarded as mutually exclusive terms, but as complementary formulations. "The Church exists both as an inclusive fellowship and as local congregations gathered for worship and Christian service. Congregations find their fulfillment in the universal community of the Church, and the universal Church exists in and through congregations. . . . In length, it acknowledges itself to be in the historic continuity of the communion of saints; in breadth, it expresses the fellowship of believers and congregations in our day" (3.02.). The church cannot be either one or the other – either local or universal – but it must be both at once, each serving and defining the other if it is to be the one, holy, catholic, and apostolic church.

With regard to its statement of purpose, the church is called to "proclaim God's saving Gospel of justification by grace for Christ's sake through faith alone, according to the apostolic witness in the Holy Scripture, preserving and transmitting the Gospel faithfully to future generations" (4.02.a.). This church acknowledges that it stands or falls in its relationship to the doctrine of justification (*articulum stantis et cadentis ecclesiae*).

On the basis of this confession of faith, the church is called upon to "carry out Christ's Great Commission by reaching out to all people . . . with a global awareness consistent with the understanding of God as Creator, Redeemer, and Sanctifier of all" (4.02.b.). This church is also to "advocate dignity and justice for all people" (4.02.c.), and to "manifest the unity given to the people of God by living together in the love of Christ and by joining with other Christians in prayer and action to express and preserve the unity which the Spirit gives" (4.02.f.). In order to fulfill these purposes, the church shall "seek unity in faith and life with all Lutherans within its boundaries and be ready to enter union negotiations whenever such unity is manifest" (4.03.d.), and "foster Christian unity by participating in ecumenical activities, contributing its witness and work and cooperating with other churches which confess God the Father, Son, and Holy Spirit" (4.03.e.).

Concerning this church's principles of organization, "this church recognizes that all power and authority in the Church belongs to the Lord Jesus Christ, its head" (5.01.). "This church, in faithfulness to the Gospel, is committed to be an inclusive church in the midst of division in society. In their organization and outreach, the congregations, synods, and churchwide units of this church shall seek to exhibit the inclusive unity that is God's will for the Church" (5.01.b.).

This church boldly reaches out in several directions simultaneously to all those with whom it may find agreement in the gospel. Each relationship will achieve levels of communion as the Spirit guides and wills since agreement with a given Christian community must proceed according to that community's set of ground rules, pursue its own historically conditioned range of issues and problems, and advance at a pace consistent with its ability to foster agreement on controverted matters and in the gospel. No two relationships will achieve unity in the same way, to the same degree, or at the same speed. This church is compelled by Scripture, creed, and confession to be reaching out to any group of Christians that confesses the Triune God, agrees in the gospel of Jesus Christ, and practices and receives the sacraments instituted by Christ. The ELCA does not commit itself only to pan-Lutheranism, pan-Protestantism, Roman Catholic rapprochement, or to developing relationships with the Orthodox. This church must reach out to all of them simultaneously, as well as to others who fit none of these categories but who profess their faith in the same Christ.

Due to its deep concern for the doctrine of justification by faith, the ELCA realizes that it must exercise genuine self-criticism, practice repentance for any past or present self-righteous and self-justifying behavior, and refrain from destructive, one-sided polemics that only serve to eliminate serious and challenging discussion. It dedicates itself with all humility and candor to seek the truth that condemns unwarranted parochialism. The ELCA, which is evangelical in its confession of faith and catholic in its concern for unity, is open to speaking a word self-critically.[4] In conformity with the doctrine of justification, the ELCA tries to avoid triumphalism and seeks unity in truth as it looks to Christ alone, grace alone, Scripture alone, and faith alone.

The ELCA understands itself to be a community of mission and witness, witness to the gospel of Jesus Christ, and mission to all nations, races, and peoples that they might believe in him. This church seeks a unity in faith, witness, and service to the gospel.

In its life of mission and witness, the ecumenical vision of the ELCA will focus on present and future theological reflection and missiological action and will not be dominated by attention to past theological controversies and divisions. Of course the witness and mission of the church can never proceed in blind disregard of its history, even the history of its scandalous disunity and mutual condemnations. Where legitimate separation might once have been necessary, current opportunities for dialogue and discussion around the central truths of faith can move the church beyond past disagreements and protracted disunity into a new situation of cooperation in witness, service, and mission.

NOTES

1. Large Catechism II in *The Book of Concord*, ed. Theodore G. Tappert (Philadelphia: Fortress Press, 1959), 33.

2. See Eugene L. Brand, *Toward a Lutheran Communion: Pulpit and Altar Fellowship*, LWF Report no. 26 (Geneva: Lutheran World Federation, 1988), 10. The LWF, at its seventh assembly, invited all churches which are committed to the Lutheran Confessions or see themselves in agreement with its doctrinal basis to become members of the communion of the LWF or enter into closer relationship with it.

3. Cf. "Statement on the Self-Understanding and Task of the Lutheran World Federation," in *Proceedings of the Seventh Assembly*, LWF Report no. 19/20 (Geneva: Lutheran World Federation, 1985), 176: "This communion is rooted in the unity of the apostolic faith as given in the Holy Scripture and witnessed by the ecumenical creeds and the Lutheran confessions."

4. "Message," in *Report of the Eighth Assembly*, Lutheran World Federation, Curitiba, Brazil, 1990 (Geneva: Lutheran World Federation, 1990).

# 7
## Forms of Ecumenism

Ecumenism must permeate, inform, and vitalize every aspect of this church's faith and life. It demonstrates the necessity for the church to be interdependent and inclusive. The interdependence among these organizational entities within this church and the inclusiveness practiced by this church in the midst of divisions in society are significant manifestations of the unity of the church. This should be evident to those within the church as well as those outside as the church pursues its mission. An extremely close relationship exists between the unity of the church and its mission (John 17:20-23).

From its evangelical, catholic, and ecumenical stance, with an obviously close relationship with mission, the Evangelical Lutheran Church in America is free to seek such forms of structure and common action as will provide true witness to Christian faith and effective expression to God's love in Christ. As congregations and synods take initiative in ecumenical activities, the whole church may learn from them. At the same time that the whole church provides policy guidance to congregations, it becomes the channel through which each congregation may minister worldwide in the whole household of faith.

The Evangelical Lutheran Church in America engages in local, regional, national and world councils of churches and other ecumenical agencies. In these relationships the Evangelical Lutheran Church in America is guided by the *evangelical* and the *representative* principles.

> The *evangelical* principle means that official membership will be established only with such ecumenical organizations as are composed exclusively

of churches which confess Jesus Christ as divine Lord and Savior. The *representative* principle means that in ecumenical organizations the official representatives of churches should never be seated on a parity with individuals who represent only themselves or organizations which are less than churches.

The Evangelical Lutheran Church in America is an active participant in bilateral and multilateral dialogues, which it does not view as competitive, but as mutually re-enforcing means for ecumenical advance. At the same time it seeks other means, such as joint efforts at mission, religious instruction, and use of the mass media to grow in understanding and agreement with other churches.

These efforts, including joint study, prayer, and worship, must be found in the various organizational expressions of the Evangelical Lutheran Church in America and other churches. All these activities need to be encouraged and to inform each other. Local ecumenism, and its synodical and regional forms, provides a rich area of progress and challenge for the unity of the church. It has much to teach and much to learn from the national and international ecumenical movement. The primary experience of ecumenism for most Christians is through their congregations, local gatherings of believers that relate to other local gatherings of other traditions, which share the same Lord, the same Baptism, the same mission.

The Evangelical Lutheran Church in America is part of a larger Lutheran community. It lives in altar and pulpit fellowship with the other member churches of the Lutheran World Federation. While its ecumenical action must be its own, it has responsibility to those churches with which it enjoys close relations to inform them of its ecumenical actions and to consider their comments and responses.

Ecumenism has as its focus and goal clarity of understanding among Christians and a greater realization of unity among Christ's people. As such it is closely related to the mission of the Gospel to all the world. It should not be confused with the important but distinct responsibility for the church to enter into conversations and reach greater understanding with people of other faiths. The Evangelical Lutheran Church in America does, in a variety of ways, engage in this inter-faith work and needs in the future, a separate, official statement to describe its commitments and aspirations in this area. When this is done, special attention must be given to the distinctiveness of Judaism.

**"Ecumenism must permeate, inform, and vitalize every aspect of this church's faith and life."** This is not an example of "ecumenical triumphalism,"[1] rather, it commits the church to conversation and dialogue with other Christians who may express the truth of the gospel differently than Lutherans. Ecumenism reflects God's desire for reconciliation of all creation and the churches' obedience to Christ's prayer that all of his followers might be one. Applied to the ELCA, it means that the church endeavors to foster a spirit of sharing tasks for Christian service. This church also strives to be inclusive because it rejoices in the gift of people of various cultures and ethnic backgrounds, recognizing the richness that diversity can bring to a community that lives according to faith in Jesus Christ.

This ecumenical dimension of the identity of the ELCA has been articulated in its constitution; ecumenically responsible witness requires pursuing a vision of ecclesial reality that is much greater than what is being experienced.

As the various expressions of the church work with one another on common tasks such as ecumenical programs, they may be tempted to relate only to those with whom they feel comfortable and who think as they do. Oneness in Jesus Christ not only calls for recognition of other points of view or the selection of church leaders who have not shared the same history; it calls for a more wholistic approach to the church and its mission – one that does not fear strangers, whoever they may be, but relates to them with sensitivity and compassion and joins with them in sharing the sorrows and joys of proclaiming Jesus Christ in the world. Ecumenism reminds the church of its essential interdependence, and of its identity as the one, holy, catholic, and apostolic church of Jesus Christ.

**"From its evangelical, catholic, and ecumenical stance, with an obviously close relationship with mission, the Evangelical Lutheran Church in America is free to seek such forms of structure and common action as will provide true witness to Christian faith and effective expression to God's love in Christ."**[2] This statement indicates that while the "true witness to Christian faith" remains the church's confessional anchor, the church may exercise a freedom with regard to ceremonies. These need not be "observed uniformly in all places." Word and sacrament unite the church to the one body, which is Christ. The church is free to seek forms, structures, and varieties of means to common action that will advance its mission and promote its witness to the gospel. If the forms and structures no longer serve this purpose, they may have to be dropped or radically reformed.

**"The primary experience of ecumenism for most Christians is through their congregations, local gatherings of believers that relate to other local gatherings of other traditions, which share the same Lord, the same Baptism, the same mission."** Both the LCA and the ALC statements on ecumenism stressed the importance of ecumenism in the congregation. The church must give "due consideration," they said, to congregational initiative and enterprise in ecumenism. The church "needs to learn from local ecumenism and offer guidance and coordination so that ecumenism in the local congregation and the ecumenical stance of the church may be in harmony." [3] The ELCA statement deepens and enhances this critically important role of the congregation in ecumenism. It perceives the role of the "whole church" as **"the channel through which each congregation may minister worldwide in the whole household of faith."** Neither the broad, catholic nature of ecumenism nor its local and particular applicability are emphasized at the expense of the other.

In its relationships with local, regional, national, and world councils of churches, the ELCA pledges itself to the "evangelical" and "representative" principles which have guided Lutherans for many years. First of all, note that these principles concern relationships with councils of churches, not with interfaith councils or ecumenical agencies whose programs are restricted to practical cooperation. Ecumenism, strictly speaking, primarily concerns the unity and common witness of the church. The ELCA participates ecumenically with "churches which confess Jesus Christ as Divine Lord and Savior." Furthermore, this church relates ecumenically only with those who are official representatives of churches and not with individuals who represent only themselves or organizations that are less than churches. In ecumenical associations this church meets with other church representatives for the purpose of achieving greater unity in witness and common service.

The evangelical and representative principles, as they apply to ecumenical relations, have their origin in the United Lutheran Church in America (ULCA) Washington Declaration of 1920, a "Declaration of Principles Concerning the Church and Its External Relationships." [4] "Every group of professing Christians calling itself a Church," it says, "will seek to express in its own life the attributes of the one, holy, catholic and apostolic Church." It does this (1) "by professing faith in Jesus Christ," (2) "by preaching the Word and administering the Sacraments," (3) "by works of serving love," and (4) "by the attempt to secure universal acceptance of the truth which it holds and confesses. Such attempts need not be accompanied by the effort to enlarge its own external organization by drawing into its membership Christians of other organizations." To accomplish these purposes, (5) "every such group will maintain the office of the ministry, commanded and instituted by Christ." [5]

Relationships with other Christians should be maintained in "the spirit of catholicity": (1) "to declare unequivocally what it believes concerning Christ and His Gospel, and to endeavor to show that it has placed the true interpretation upon that Gospel . . . and to testify definitely and frankly against error"; (2) "to approach others without hostility, jealousy, suspicion or pride, in the sincere and humble desire to give and receive Christian service"; (3) "to grant cordial recognition of all agreements which are discovered between its own interpretation of the Gospel and that which others hold"; and (5) "to cooperate with other Christians in works of serving love . . . insofar as this can be done without surrender of its interpretation of the Gospel, without denial of conviction, and without suppression of its testimony as to what it holds to be the truth."[6]

With regard to union with other Lutherans, the ULCA "recognized no doctrinal reason against complete cooperation and organic union with such bodies."[7] With regard to Protestants, "we hold the union of Christians in a single organization to be of less importance than the agreement of Christians in the proclamation of the Gospel." The Washington Declaration stated an "earnest desire to cooperate with other Church Bodies . . . provided, that such co-operation does not involve the surrender of our interpretation of the Gospel." Blanket approval of all cooperative movements was withheld, "since we hold that co-operation is not an end in itself."[8] Nine principles were proposed as the basis for practical cooperation: (1) "the Fatherhood of God, revealed in His son Jesus Christ"; (2) "the true Godhead of Jesus Christ"; (3) "the continued activity of God the Holy Spirit among men"; (4) "the supreme importance of the Word of God and the Sacraments"; (5) the authority of the Old and New Testaments," as the rule and standard by which all doctrines and teachers are to be judged"; (6) "the reality and universality of sin"; (7) "the love, and the righteousness of God, Who for Christ's sake, bestows forgiveness and righteousness upon all who believe in Christ"; (8) "the present existence upon earth of the kingdom of God . . . as a spiritual reality and an object of faith"; (9) and "the hope of Christ's second coming."[9] The church cannot enter into any organization or movement that denies any of these doctrines, or limits the cooperating churches in their confession of the truth. Nor can the church cooperate in movements or organizations "whose activities lie outside the proper sphere of Church activity." "In determining what that sphere is, we must be guided by the fundamental principle of the Word, the administration of the Sacraments, and the performance of works of love. . . . We hold that the use of the Church . . . as an agency for the enactment and enforcement of law, or for the application of other methods of external force, is foreign to the true purpose for which the Church exists."[10]

E. Theodore Bachmann reminds us that the targets for most of these principles and restrictions was the Federal Council of Churches and the Sunday School Council of Religious Education. The modern reader must also be aware of the threat that Fundamentalism and the Social Gospel movement posed to evangelical Christianity. Bachmann says the Federal Council's updating of its commitment to the "Social Creed of the Churches" in 1919 was seen as symptomatic of a prevailing condition.[11]

The final section of the declaration deals with movements and organizations "injurious to the Christian faith." These include groups that deny the reality of sin, the divinity of Christ, the redemption of the world by Christ's suffering and death, and the truth and authority of Scripture. "We therefore lay it upon the consciences of pastors and the members of all our congregations to scrutinize with the utmost care the doctrines and principles of all teachers, sects, organizations and societies . . . which seek their adherence and support."[12] This section, Bachmann writes, "carries implied admonition to United Lutheran Church in America pastors and laity to avoid membership in secret societies, notably Freemasonry, or any others practicing a quasi-religious ritual."[13]

This statement formed the basis for the evangelical and representative principles that guided the ULCA until well into the post-World War II era. But if the LCA could trace its ecumenical lineage to the Washington Declaration of 1920, the ALC's antecedents run back to the Chicago Theses, presented to the National Lutheran Council in 1919.[14] The Chicago Theses declare that "the Lutheran Church believes that in all essentials, it is the Apostolic Church, with the Word of God in its purity and the Sacraments as instituted by our Lord."[15] Its members are to attend services in their own churches, have their children baptized by their own pastors, receive Holy Communion at their own altars, and "pulpit and altar fellowship with pastors and people of other confessions are to be avoided, as contrary to a true and consistent Lutheranism."[16]

The Chicago Theses were followed by the Minneapolis Theses in 1925, which provided the basis for the formation of The American Lutheran Church in 1930 and the American Lutheran Conference. The Minneapolis Theses declared that "where the establishment and maintenance of church fellowship ignores present doctrinal differences or declares them a matter of indifference, there is unionism, pretense of union which does not exist."[17] It also agreed with the Galesburg Rule.

Ralph Long (1882-1948) became secretary of the American Section of the Lutheran World Convention in 1935. Long served as one of two Lutheran delegates to the Utrecht meeting of the Provisional Committee of the WCC in Process of Formation, a move that ran counter to the prevailing sentiment regarding ecumenism in the ALC.[18] Nevertheless, in 1944 the old ALC became a charter member of the World Council of Churches, as did the ULCA in 1948 (the ELC joined in 1956). The new ALC voted to become a member in 1960.

International Lutheran unity after World War II and the formation of the WCC posed a monumental challenge to Lutheranism. Bachmann expresses it in the following manner:

> Having attained confessional representation, what would Lutheran churches make of it? Would it be regarded as an end in itself, as a bulwark of confessionalism? Or would it become a means to an end, a motivation to strive for a manifested unity of Christians in the Gospel? Had not the latter been the intention of the Lutheran Confessions? The Reformers and even earlier proponents of Lutheran orthodoxy always presupposed the Church catholic and evangelical as fact and challenge.[19]

After World War II Lutherans in North America entered into ecumenical relations purposefully, especially in the person of Franklin Clark Fry (1900-68), president of the ULCA since 1944 who, with Augustana's President Bersell, sat on the World Council's Central Committee. Fry served as vice-chair[man].

Fry and the ULCA were also active in the formation of the NCCC but entered into the relationship cautiously. In 1947, for instance, scrutinizing the proposed constitution for a national council, the ULCA, which maintained a consultative relationship with the Federal Council, surfaced two fundamental difficulties: it made possible "admission into membership churches and agencies whose evangelical character is not clearly established; it provides for rather inclusive cooperation of personnel not representative of the churches as such."[20] The ULCA also sought changes in the preamble to the proposed constitution, relating Christian unity directly to Christ. As Bachmann says, "In the sense that Christology determines ecclesiology, so also ecclesiology determines the relations of churches to each other when they seek to cooperate as churches and not simply as religious agencies. From this premise, as already set forth in the Washington Declaration, flow two unvarying principles: the evangelical and the representative."[21]

Fry reiterated the evangelical and representative principles in his 1946 presidential report to the ULCA convention. He went back to the Washington Declaration for an exposition of the evangelical principle; for the representative principle, to the 1922 convention's approval of a statement by the Executive Board with respect to ULCA association with the Federal Council. The Board declared that the ULCA "cannot authorize any relationship on the part of Synods, Boards, pastors, congregations or societies which would compromise loyalty to its confessional positions."[22] This meant that "church must meet church" through "representatives that represent."[23] Fry added this positive corollary: "The United Lutheran Church must be prepared to go where these correct principles lead."

The evangelical and representative principles represent the Lutheran contribution to the modern conciliar movement, since they were incorporated into the NCCC at the urging of the ULCA.

In 1954, as directed by the 1950 convention, the Executive Board's guidelines concerning principles governing interdenominational relationships were approved by the Toronto convention. The evangelical and representative principles were spelled out in detail.[24] Local councils were urged to conform the preamble of their constitutions to the National Council's. ULCA congregations and pastors were to "enter into official connection only with denominational agencies composed exclusively of evangelical churches. No deviation from this principle ought to occur."[25]

These principles were reiterated when the LCA was formed. Accordingly, the Executive Board gave direction to its synods, urging the evangelical and representative principles. At the 1964 convention these were submitted for adoption.

> The *evangelical* principle means that official relationship with interchurch agencies will be established only with such agencies as are composed exclusively of churches which confess Jesus Christ as Divine Lord and Savior.
> The *representative* principle means that in interchurch associations the official representatives of churches should never be expected to sit on a parity with individuals who represent only themselves or at most organizations which are less than churches.[26]

Also in 1964, at the Second General Convention of the ALC, the following resolution was adopted:

> In all interchurch relationships, we approve what has been termed the "evangelical principle" and the "representative principle" namely, that official relationship with interchurch agencies will be established only with such agencies as are composed exclusively of churches which confess Jesus Christ as divine Lord and Saviour; and in interchurch associations the official representatives of churches should never be expected to sit on a parity with individuals who represent only themselves or at most organizations which are less than churches.[27]

**"The ELCA is an active participant in bilateral and multilateral dialogues, which it does not view as competitive, but as mutually re-enforcing means for ecumenical advance."** The immediate goals of bilateral and multilateral dialogue are similar. They seek the lifting of specific mutual condemnations, convergence if not consensus on matters of basic Christian doctrine, and the reception of the results of the dialogues.

They are "mutually re-enforcing means." They frequently treat the same topics and seek in harmony to advance the unity of the church. These dialogues are closely related to local ecumenism and endeavor to promote it. Local ecumenism in turn promotes and influences the work of the dialogues. The local congregation affords numerous occasions for Christians to live out "the joyous experience of the unity of Christ's people." Joining with others in prayer, study, and worship, they celebrate the unity that God has given to the church. In this way they also anticipate the unity that God promises to those who call upon the name of the Lord.

The ELCA as a whole is also a "local" church, inasmuch as it relates to the "larger Lutheran community." A specific form of relationship is mentioned: the ELCA "lives in altar and pulpit fellowship with the other member churches of the Lutheran World Federation." Debate is currently under way concerning Lutheran ecclesiology. This includes an analysis of "pulpit and altar fellowship," and the implications of such fellowship for a worldwide Lutheran "communion."[28]

The struggles over the precise definition of what it means to achieve communion within the one church of Jesus Christ do not affect this church's relations with other faiths in the same way. Interfaith and interchurch relations must be distinguished from each other, though this effort at precision in no way seeks to limit ELCA involvement in interfaith conversations. The distinction only serves to clarify the scope and range of these respective activities. Ecumenism, properly speaking, is concerned with the unity and witness of the church. A separate statement will be necessary to govern interfaith relationships. In that process, "special attention must be given to the distinctiveness of Judaism."

## NOTES

1. C. Jack Eichorst, "Reflections on the Proposed Statement on Ecumenism for the First Assembly of the ELCA," *Responses to the Proposed Statement on Ecumenism of the Evangelical Lutheran Church in America* (Chicago: Office of Ecumenical Affairs, 1989). Cf. response by Clarence Solberg: "The opening sentence . . . is a bit too strong, may even be grandiose"; and that of Roger W. Fjeld: "We plead . . . for a statement more modest in its understanding of ecumenism in the life and mission of the Church."

2. On the term, "evangelical catholic," see E. Theodore Bachmann, *The Ecumenical Involvement of the LCA Predecessor Bodies: A Brief History 1900-1962*, rev. 2d ed. (New York: Division for World Mission and Ecumenism, Lutheran Church in America, 1983), 37-41. It was on the basis of evangelical catholicity that Nathan Söderblom spoke of the "organic unity" of the church. In an address at Philadelphia Seminary in 1924 he said: "Evangelic Catholicity means to me not only a historic fact, but also the only direction in which organic unity can be reached." Söderblom concluded: "The Catholicity of the Church cannot be accomplished and fulfilled as long as formalistic or nomistic conditions are deemed to be necessary for salvation or for Chris-

tian unity. Only our pure Evangelic doctrine of salvation through trust in God is able to rally the Christian communions with their manifold divergences of worship, church-order and tradition into one signal fellowship, one organic unity" (quoted in Bachmann, 39). American Lutherans were not as convinced that organic unity was the appropriate goal of Evangelical Catholicity (39-40); and it was left to Augustana professor Conrad Bergendoff to give Söderblom's ecclesiology a firmer Christological foundation. Bergendoff's contribution in this regard was the preamble to the LCA constitution (40). Thus, Evangelical Catholicity was a concept that underwent a process of development as it attempted to hold to the Lutheran confessional center, while remaining open to the one church in all its diversity. See also the Washington Declaration (192) in Richard C. Wolf, ed., *Documents of Lutheran Unity in America* (Philadelphia: Fortress Press, 1966), no. 148, 346-50.

3. *Ecumenism: A Lutheran Commitment* (New York: Lutheran Church in America, 1982), IV, 12; *Ecumenical Perspective and Guidelines* (Minneapolis: The American Lutheran Church, 1985) IV, 9.

4. Wolf, *Documents*, no. 148, 346-55. For a discussion concerning the Washington Declaration, see Bachmann, *Ecumenical Involvement*, 26-35, 43. The Washington Declaration created an impact upon the ecumenical world. Upon receipt of the declaration, Secretary Gardiner, of the Faith and Order movement, wrote President Knubel of the ULCA: "If you could send me six copies I think I could use them to great advantage. . . . The Declaration is so entirely in harmony with our hopes and purposes of the World Conference movement" (43). The position of the ULCA, based on the Washington Declaration, helped to influence the "Declaration by Members of the Lutheran Communion," urging restraint on overly hasty infatuation at the Lausanne Conference on Faith and Order in 1927. See Bachmann, *Ecumenical Involvement*, 49-50. In 1922 the ULCA voted in convention to only go as far as a consultative relationship with Federal Council of Churches. Then at the 1924 convention of the ULCA action was taken to relate officially to Faith and Order and Life and Work. Augustana decided to relate only to Life and Work, while the Norwegian Lutheran Church in America and the Lutheran Free Church each sent one delegate to the Faith and Order Conference at Lausanne in 1927. See Bachmann, *Ecumenical Involvement*, 44-49.

5. Wolf, *Documents*, 348-49.

6. Wolf, *Documents*, 350.

7. See note 6 above.

8. Wolf, *Documents*, 351-52.

9. Wolf, *Documents*, 352-53.

10. Wolf, *Documents*, 353.

11. Bachmann, *Ecumenical Involvement*, 30-31.

12. Wolf, *Documents*, 354.

13. Bachmann, *Ecumenical Involvement*, 33.

14. Bachmann, *Ecumenical Involvement*, Appendix: "the 'Chicago Theses,' authored by [Hans] Stub in 1919, and the 'Washington Declaration' authored by the United Lutheran Church in America's Knubel and Jacobs in 1920, remain as the readiest

examples of the guarded route to Lutheran unity, on the one hand, and the open route on the other."

15. Wolf, *Documents*, 300.

16. Wolf, *Documents*, 301.

17. Wolf, *Documents*, 241.

18. Bachmann, *Ecumenical Involvement*, Appendix, 16-18.

19. Bachmann, *Ecumenical Involvement*, 84.

20. Quoted in Bachmann, *Ecumenical Involvement*, 90.

21. Bachmann, *Ecumenical Involvement*, 92.

22. Bachmann, *Ecumenical Involvement*, 98.

23. See note 22 above.

24. Bachmann, *Ecumenical Involvement*, 108.

25. See note 24 above.

26. These principles were reaffirmed by the LCA in 1974 and included in the LCA statement, *Ecumenism: A Lutheran Commitment.* Bachmann adds, quoting the LCA "Guide to Principles Governing Interdenominational Relationships of LCA Congregations and their Auxiliaries" (1968), 135: "When such cooperation does not take the form of official interchurch relations, neither the evangelical principle nor the representative principle need apply." The evangelical and representative principles were also adopted by the ALC. See *Reports and Actions of the Second General Convention* (1964), 677; and the ALC statement, *Ecumenical Perspective and Guidelines*, 12-13. The latter ALC document, however, restates the evangelical principle (12). It declares that the ALC adheres "to the evangelical principle whereby we recognize no other way of salvation than the way provided by the Triune God for the redemption of all mankind, accomplished through Jesus Christ in his death and resurrection, and conveyed by the Spirit of God in and through the Gospel in Word and Sacrament."

27. 1964 *Reports and Actions*, 677.

28. See Eugene L. Brand, *Toward a Lutheran Communion: Pulpit and Altar Fellowship*, LWF Report no. 26 (Geneva: Lutheran World Federation, 1988).

# 8
## Goal and Stages of Relationships

The Evangelical Lutheran Church in America is an active participant in the ecumenical movement, because of its desire for Christian unity. Its goal is full communion, i.e., the full or complete realization of unity with all those churches that confess the Triune God. The Evangelical Lutheran Church in America, both as a church and as a member of the wider communion of churches in the Lutheran World Federation, seeks to reach this goal.

Full communion will be a gift from God and will be founded on faith in Jesus Christ. It will be a commitment to truth in love and a witness to God's liberation and reconciliation. Full communion will be visible and sacramental. It is obviously a goal towards which divided churches, under God's Spirit, are striving, but which has not been reached. It is also a goal in need of continuing definition. It will be rooted in agreement on essentials and allow diversity in nonessentials.

However, in most cases the churches will not be able to move immediately from their disunity to a full expression of their God-given unity, but can expect to experience a movement from disunity to unity that may include one or more of the following stages of relationships.

1. Ecumenical Cooperation. Here the Evangelical Lutheran Church in America enters into ecumenical relations based on the *evangelical* and *representative* principles.
2. Bilateral and Multilateral Dialogues. Here the Evangelical Lutheran Church in America enters into dialogues, with varying mandates, with those who agree with the evangelical and representative prin-

ciples, confess the Triune God, and share a commitment to "ecumenical conversion." This conversion or repentance includes openness to new possibilities under the guidance of God's Spirit.

3. Preliminary Recognition. Here the Evangelical Lutheran Church in America can be involved on a church-to-church basis in eucharistic sharing and cooperation, without exchangeability of ministers.

   a. One stage requires 1 and 2 above, plus partial, mutual recognition of church and sacraments with partial agreement in doctrine.

   b. A second stage requires 1, 2, and 3a, partial and mutual recognition of ordained ministers and of churches, fuller agreement in doctrine, commitments to work for full communion, and preliminary agreement on lifting of any mutual condemnations.

4. Full Communion. At this stage the goal of the involvement of this church in the ecumenical movement has been fully attained. Here the question of the shape and form of full communion needs to be addressed and answered in terms of what will best further the mission of the Church in individual cases.

For the Evangelical Lutheran Church in America, the characteristics of full communion will include at least the following, some of which will exist at earlier stages:

1. a common confessing of the Christian faith;
2. a mutual recognition of Baptism and a sharing of the Lord's Supper, allowing for an exchangeability of members;
3. a mutual recognition and availability of ordained ministers to the service of all members of churches in full communion, subject only but always to the disciplinary regulations of the other churches;
4. a common commitment to evangelism, witness, and service;
5. a means of common decision making on critical common issues of faith and life;
6. a mutual lifting of any condemnations that exist between churches.

This definition of full communion is understood to be consistent with Article VII of the Augsburg Confession, which says, "for the true unity of the church it is enough to agree concerning the teaching of the Gospel and the administration of the sacraments." Agreement in the Gospel can be reached and stated without adopting Lutheran confessional formulations as such. This definition is also in agreement with the understanding of unity adopted by the Seventh Assembly of the Lutheran World Federation in 1984, "The Unity We Seek" (quoted under the Lutheran World Federation section of this statement).

## Conclusion
**The Evangelical Lutheran Church in America seeks to be faithful to its scriptural and confessional foundations. As a church that is evangelical, catholic, and ecumenical, this church will pursue the goal of full communion and will rejoice in movement toward that goal.**

The expressed goal of ecumenism, according to the statement, is said to be full communion,[1] defined as **"the full or complete realization of unity with all those churches that confess the Triune God."** Full communion cannot be attained at once or immediately, but deliberately and gradually in **"a movement from disunity to unity."** This unity is **"visible and sacramental"** and may include one or more of the following stages of relationships: ecumenical cooperation, bilateral and multilateral dialogues, preliminary recognition, and full communion. The statement acknowledges that full communion is **"a goal in need of continuing definition."** While a goal that must be **"rooted in agreement on essentials,"** it will **"allow diversity in nonessentials."**[2] Full communion does not imply the creation of a "mega-church,"[3] though its extent cannot be limited.[4]

The statement adds what it considers to be minimal criteria for full communion: **"(1) a common confessing of the Christian faith; (2) a mutual recognition of Baptism and a sharing of the Lord's Supper, allowing for an exchangeability of members; (3) a mutual recognition and availability of ordained ministers . . . ; (4) a common commitment to evangelism, witness, and service; (5) a means of common decision making . . . ; and (6) a mutual lifting of any condemnations that exist between churches."**

These criteria attempt to define minimally what the statement acknowledges to be a rather fluid concept. The term full communion is still in the process of being defined. If the basis for full communion is always the proclamation of the gospel and the administration of the sacraments, the rest may be negotiable. Far from closing off debate, the consideration of Word and sacrament as the foundation of full communion ought to make possible both discussion and actual progress towards greater visible unity. Such a basis should provoke churches into accepting the gift of unity and taking seriously the command to work toward that end. As the ALC statement on ecumenism states, "the unity of church is a *gift*, given by God as part of that new community created by faith in the Gospel; and the unity of the church is also a *task* as Christians and churches seek to manifest that which God has given."[5]

Full communion does not prescribe certain fixed forms and models of unity. The church, gathered around Word and sacrament, continually struggles to live out its faith. This was apparent to the framers of the *Niagara*

*Report: Report of the Anglican-Lutheran Consultation on Episcope 1987.* "We recognize that one of our tasks must be the rethinking and reformulating of the meaning of 'full communion.' We are persuaded that such reformulation can take place only in the context of our growing common experience with one another."[6] Full communion is a dynamic concept requiring constant critique and redefinition within the context of the church's ongoing struggle to accept and achieve visible, tangible unity. In this sense it has remained, and undoubtedly always will remain, a problematic goal. *Facing Unity: Models, Forms and Phases of Catholic-Lutheran Church Fellowship* (1985) puts it this way:

> Reconciliation is not possible without dialogue and constant communication. It is a process of discerning the spirits and of searching for steps along a pathway known only to God. Reconciliation is thus a dynamic process, even where church unity exists or has been re-established. For as long as sin and conflict remain and as long as Christians and churches live in changing times and in a diverse world, this process will not be completed.[7]

Over the years numerous bilateral dialogues have regarded full communion not only as a concept in need of critique and further definition but also as the goal their conversations eventually wish to achieve. The *Report of the Preparatory Group for International Level Lutheran/Orthodox Dialogue* (1978) offered full communion as the "ultimate goal":

> Because of the command of our Lord that the church be one we are convinced that the ultimate goal of the Lutheran/Orthodox dialogue can be nothing less than full *communion as mutual recognition.* The ultimate goal of full communion is not to be seen as merely an inter-ecclesiastical goal but one inseparable from a common witness informed by the apostolic vision and mission pointed to the salvation and unity of all humankind. It is the conviction of the Lutheran Preparatory Group that a detailed description of the meaning of full communion is the task of the dialogue itself.[8]

The *Anglican-Lutheran Dialogue: The Report of the European Commission* (1982) stated: "There are no longer any obstacles on the way towards the establishment of full communion between our two Churches." Remaining differences "of theological emphasis" are not serious enough to be divisive, "though we recognize that our agreement needs to be tested and received by the Churches."[9]

In *Facing Unity*, the subject of full communion is predicated not just on agreement concerning, but the actual sharing of, a common life in Word and sacrament. The text phrases it in the following way:

> Community with Christ and community of Christians with each other are mediated through word and sacrament in the Holy Spirit. Where Christians

and churches desire full community [*Gemeinschaft*] with each other, it follows that their joint understanding of the apostolic witness and their common testimony to the Christian faith . . . must go hand in hand with a common sacramental life.[10]

Full communion relates directly to visible unity. Such is the stated goal of the Commission on Faith and Order of the WCC. As written in the preface to BEM:

> The Commission has been charged by the Council members to keep always before them their accepted obligation to work towards manifesting more visibly God's gift of Church unity. So it is that the stated aim of the Commission is "to proclaim the oneness of the Church of Jesus Christ and to call the churches to the goal of visible unity in one faith and one eucharistic fellowship, expressed in worship and common life in Christ, in order that the world might believe."[11]

If full communion, as the visible unity of the church, will not happen all at once, it will have to occur through stages; "the goal of 'full communion' is achieved through a process."[12] "Like any other endeavor, this struggle for church unity needs conceptions of its goal – even if they can only be provisional in character – if it is to achieve direction, strength, and permanence."[13]

The preparatory group for international level Lutheran/Orthodox dialogue said it learned that all steps in the process of engaging in bilateral dialogue are steps towards the recognition and the realization of the given unity of the church. A few years later the international Roman Catholic/Lutheran Joint Commission published a document titled *Ways to Community*,[14] which was divided into two parts: "Unity as Goal" and "Steps Toward Unity." It gave the following rationale for the preparation of the document:

> In the course of its work the Joint Commission came to the conclusion that, if there were to be any further progress in inter-church relationships, clarity was needed and a certain measure of agreement, both about the goal (Part I) and about concrete steps towards unity (Part II). A bird's eye view is necessary if we are to see how the various themes discussed in the dialogue and the tasks set us for cooperation fit into the total picture, lest we find ourselves speaking and acting at cross purposes and misunderstanding one another.[15]

The same commission then studied the question of ministry, and in the document *The Ministry in the Church* emphasized that recognition can only come about gradually. "The various stages lead from a mutual respect of ministries through practical cooperation to full recognition of the ministry of the other church which is identical to the acceptance of eucharistic fellowship."[16]

As churches move in the direction of greater visible unity, steps and stages offer necessary interim assistance and much-needed clarification. Stages function both as a breathing space during which to check and refine the unity thus far received and as a position from which to move on to greater unity. Since the goal of full communion is itself in constant need of redefinition, then the working out of stages to fellowship is a necessary and fundamental component of that process.

This is true especially with regard to multilateral dialogue, which, by its very nature, must address a more complex set of traditions. The BEM text of 1982 puts it this way:

> On the way towards their goal of visible unity . . . the churches will have to pass through various stages. . . . In the process of growing together in mutual trust, the churches must develop these doctrinal convergences step by step, until they are living in communion with one another in continuity with the apostles and the teachings of the universal Church.[17]

BEM, as the multilateral document *par excellence*, considers that the discussion related to the document is a fundamental part of this process. An important distinction must be made between the goal and purpose of bilateral and multilateral discussions. The more narrowly focused bilateral dialogues can make concrete suggestions for overcoming specific barriers and uncover and achieve important convergence as they move toward greater unity; multilateral agreements must work at a slower pace and maintain a wider perspective as they set their sights on the more modest goal of preliminary recognition. As the following quotation indicates, the goal of BEM is preliminary recognition as a crucial step along the path toward full communion:

> In the course of critical evaluation the primary purposes of this ecumenical text must be kept in mind. Readers should not expect to find a complete theological treatment of baptism, eucharist and ministry. That would be neither appropriate nor desirable here. The agreed text purposely concentrates on those aspects of the theme that have been directly or indirectly related to the problems of mutual recognition leading to unity.[18]

Some bilateral dialogues propose specific steps by which full communion may be achieved. The *Anglican-Lutheran Dialogue* (European Commission) in 1982 proposed "interim steps towards full communion."[19] The *Lutheran Episcopal Agreement*, which preceded the European dialogue (1982), had already proposed interim eucharistic sharing. It declared that the churches were "looking forward to the day when full communion is established between Anglican and Lutheran Churches."[20] *Facing Unity*, a follow-up to *Ways to Community*, was written for the purpose of proposing and suggesting specific models and stages of progress towards the unity of Lutherans and Roman Catholics. Part II is titled, "Forms and Phases of Catholic-Lutheran Fellowship," part of which reads as follows:

> The dynamic inherent in the process of reconciliation and the realization of church fellowship unfolds itself more clearly in the efforts for (a) fellowship in confessing the one apostolic faith (community of faith), (b) fellowship in sacramental life (community in sacraments), (c) fellowship as a structured fellowship in which community of faith and community of sacraments find adequate ecclesial form and in which common life, common decisions and common action are not only possible; they are required (community of service)."[21]

While *Facing Unity* presupposes a visible form of unity – "the unity we seek must assume concrete form in suitable structures"[22] – this unity is no mere uniformity. Thus, "Reformation theology reiterates the conviction that complete conformity is not a condition for church unity."[23]

Also, the so-called Meissen report of the Church of England, the Bund der Evangelischen Kirchen in der Deutschen Demokratischen Republik, and the Evangelische Kirche in Deutschland, *On the Way to Visible Unity: A Common Statement* (1988), recognizes the goal of their ecumenical relations as "growth towards full, visible unity." "Perfect unity," it says, "must await the final coming of God's Kingdom." But in a fallen world, "we are committed to strive for the 'full, visible unity' of the body of Christ on earth." The churches pledge themselves "to work for the manifestation of unity at every level, a unity which is grounded in the life of the Holy Trinity and is God's purpose for the whole creation." "Full, visible unity" will include: a common confession of faith; the sharing of one baptism; the celebrating of one Eucharist; and the service of a reconciled, common ministry. These bonds of communion enable the church to "guard and interpret the apostolic faith, to take decisions, to teach authoritatively, to share goods and to bear effective witness in the world."[24] Section VI is titled "Mutual acknowledgement and next steps," whereby the churches "commit [them]-selves to strive together for full, visible unity."[25]

It might be argued that "the concept 'full communion' is articulated in the interests of ecumenical engagement with the episcopally governed communions to which doctrines of ministry and episkope are essential."[26] Recent ecumenical developments do not bear this out. *Toward Church Fellowship*, the report of the Joint Commission of the Lutheran World Federation and the World Alliance of Reformed Churches,[27] speaks specifically about visible unity and the stages necessary to achieve full communion in the following paragraphs:

> We rejoice that some Lutheran and Reformed churches have already declared church fellowship with churches of the other tradition. . . . We encourage

other churches to confirm for themselves the reality of their unity in Christ through such a declaration of full communion.

We call upon all Lutheran and Reformed churches to make their unity more real and visible to their members and to the world. Whether a church is taking its first steps of rapprochement or has already declared church fellowship with the other tradition, continuing growth in unity will be a faithful response to Christ's will for unity. As intentional continuing steps in realizing our unity, we encourage the churches: To take the initiative in reaching out to the other. . . . To engage in ongoing theological work and reflection together on the central doctrines of our faith. . . . To develop a common witness and service to the world. . . . To incorporate learning about the fellowship between our churches into our total educational program. . . . To work out whatever new common organizational structures may be necessary for the sake of witness to the new relationship. To carry out the actions mentioned above in ways that are consonant with our commitments to other churches in the larger ecumenical movement.[28]

The visible unity of the church is realized in full communion, which includes more than pulpit and altar fellowship. However, some disagree. "Instead of 'full communion,'" one theologian writes, "we might use the characteristic Lutheran term 'pulpit and altar fellowship,' or the older term 'table fellowship,' or we might invent a new and more fully descriptive designation for this reality."[29] As Eugene Brand has written, "Pulpit and altar fellowship are essential, even basic, to communio, but communio (*koinonia*) is both broader and deeper."[30] Brand further develops an understanding of the Lutheran approach to communio along the lines laid down by CA VII. The LWF has argued for an ecclesiological understanding:

While it is true that CA7 constitutes a break with the medieval concept of the church as a grace-dispensing institution, the break is made precisely in the interest of restoring a biblical, patristic communio ecclesiology. Concentration on the *satis est* should not overshadow the point of departure of CA7: "(ein heilige christliche Kirche) ist die Versammlung aller Gläubigen. . . . " (One holy Christian church) is the assembly of all believers. . . . The church is not individuals, the church is a "gathering (assembly) of people" – "not the persons simply as such, but something that happens with them, as the concrete occurrence of their reality as a community."[31]

This has implications for Lutheran participation in the *oikomene*:

In developing such an ecclesiology it has never been the Lutheran intention to limit communion in a sectarian manner. Quite the contrary. It has rather been to see the Lutheran communion as a vital participant in the total *communio sanctorum*, actively joining the struggle to realize more perfectly the communion given in Christ. This posture has deep roots in the Lutheran heritage. In the Large Catechism's exposition of the creed, Luther makes the connection between communion and unity. And in his 1519 treatise on the Eucharist he links sacramental communion with ecclesial communion.[32]

Brand raises the crucial question of CA VII and what is sufficient (*satis est*) for full communion. How one interprets the terms "full communion," "stages to fellowship," and "visible unity" as used in this document will depend on the interpretation one gives to *satis est*.

Over the years Lutherans have discussed the manner and extent to which the unity of the church ought to be pursued in certain given historical circumstances. In this regard, the current discussion is the most recent manifestation of a historical debate. One view suggests that: "The *satis est* is really nothing more than a statement about the eschatological limit to our ecclesiologies. The gospel is the end, the 'full communion.' There is nothing more."[33] Another view is that the *satis est* is "not opposed to the demand of the 'fullness' of church life but actually opens up the way to this fullness."[34]

Some Lutherans have regarded the conditions of unity expressed in CA VII as the fulfillment of full communion; others consider it the beginning that opens up the process whereby full communion may be achieved. For the former, full communion implies additional and unnecessary requirements beyond CA VII; for the latter, full communion includes certain characteristics inherent in CA VII. These opinions reflect two of a variety of positions that exist in this discussion. In view of these significant deliberations, the Standing Committee of the Office for Ecumenical Affairs requested the Institute for Ecumenical Research in Strasbourg to give an opinion on the relationship of Article VII of the Augsburg Confession to the concept of full communion. The opinion appears in this volume as Appendix 1. *Ecumenism: The Vision of the Evangelical Lutheran Church in America* opts for an interpretation of CA VII that includes stages.

The description of the unity of the church found in CA VII has been taken seriously in the various multi- and bilateral dialogues in which Lutherans have played a major role. A defensive posture, once necessary and legitimately supported by appeals to CA VII, has given way to an attitude of critical openness in recent years. A fresh interpretation of CA VII, emerging in part from the ecumenical dialogue, has propelled many Lutherans in this new direction.

Movement of the churches from disunity to visible unity involves a series of stages that are lived out at different times and in different ways in relationship to other churches. These stages are part of a spectrum ranging from disunity to visible unity. The stages in ecumenical relationships reflect and confirm the increasing convergence of churches on doctrinal matters. This convergence raises the question of the possibility of common structures and shared resources among churches. For example, increased theological agreement has fostered collaboration among the faculties of theological seminaries. Again, the interim eucharistic sharing with Episcopalians has made possible a limited sharing of ministry in the context of worship.

In describing the characteristics of full communion, the ELCA statement on ecumenism builds upon the sharing of ministry when it speaks of "a mutual recognition and availability of ordained ministers" (14). The statement also makes the modest proposal for "a means of common decision making on critical common issues of faith and life" (14). In these ways the doctrinal convergence that marks our ecumenical era translates into mutual recognition and shared responsibility.

Does this mean that the churches are headed for a single structure, a sort of "megachurch"? Not at all. Visible unity does not have to mean merger. The heart of the Lutheran teaching in CA VII is this: the unity of the church is not dependent upon a structurally uniform organization. The unity of the church is dependent only upon the faithfulness of the church to the gospel. For Lutherans, this opens the possibility of a plurality of structures that respond to the call for evangelical preaching. Consequently, the historical, structural, and administrative aspect of the church's organization remains open to variety and cooperation, to diversity, and to mutual recognition, to multiple expressions of the church's being, and to shared responsibility in its functioning.[35] While the progress of living out unity will inevitably involve different phases or stages for the churches, the list presented in *Ecumenism: The Vision of the Evangelical Lutheran Church in America* is not intended to be either rigid or exhaustive. Nor should it be viewed as strictly chronological. There may be overlapping of stages. For example, dialogues and preliminary forms of recognition may exist simultaneously. As the language of *Ecumenism* indicates, the suggested stages add nothing to the teaching of Article VII of the Augsburg Confession, but they are a general description of how churches finding agreement in the teaching of the gospel and the administration of the sacraments will visibly reflect this agreement in their lives and teaching. The "stages of relationships" is an approximate blueprint of a movement of churches for coexistence, in some cases competition, to communion. It is a depiction of how churches will discover, and be given, the agreement described in Article VII, so that it will affect their lives and relations with each other. The models in which full communion would be lived out would vary depending on the partner and would include various polities. The characteristics of full communion given in the statement are not a complete or a static definition but represent a current ecumenical consensus.[36]

NOTES

1. For a better understanding of this expression and concept, see Appendix 3 in this volume, which is a dossier on the term "full communion" prepared by Michael Root at the request of the Office for Ecumenical Affairs, ELCA.

2. See especially Luther Northwestern Seminary's "faculty response to ELCA Ecumenical Document," in *Responses to the Proposed Statement on Ecumenism of the Evangelical Lutheran Church in America*. It states five objections to the term "full communion": "(1) The term 'full communion' connotes strategy and program rather than policy. (2) It seems to make certain structural requirements that deny the inclusive understanding of CA VII. (3) It has associations with particular Christian traditions and may tilt our ecumenical participation in a certain direction. (4) The term is not understood uniformly by all Christians. (5) The exclusive use of the term is premature in light of the ongoing ELCA study of ministry." Cf. response by John Hotchkin: "The importance in maintaining communion as the fundamental reality is that it provides the basis for standards and criteria which enable us to go beyond a superficial and uncritical tolerance of differences to truly reconciled and transformed diversities."

3. See *The Niagara Report: Report of the Anglican-Lutheran Consultation on Episcope* (London: Anglican Consultative Council; Geneva: Lutheran World Federation, 1968), 44: " 'Full communion', the consequence of such acknowledgment and recognition does not mean the organizational merger of the Anglican and Lutheran Churches." But the fear that full communion might mean just that was expressed by several critics. See the following responses in *Responses to the Proposed Statement:* Ronald Coen ("Throughout the document there seems to be an underlying understanding that the entire purpose of the ecumenical movement is that of having a single church structure."); Gerhard Forde (The goal of full communion is "the end product of a confusion between the unity which is given only as a gift through Christ and the gospel, the communio sanctorum, and more visible and structural union. . . . 'Full communion' is and remains a gift of God in Christ. . . . When one speaks so grandly about 'full communion' as the goal one runs the risk once again of transcending the eschatological barriers. No ecumenical strategy can create 'full communion.' More eschatological modesty is needed. . . . The temptation all along in the insistence on visible unity is to obscure the eschatological limit to our claims and structures. It is precisely to think we can achieve institutionally something more than the gospel grants. . . . The gospel is the end, the 'full communion.' There is nothing more."); Todd Nichol ("Arguably, the concept 'full communion' is articulated in the interests of ecumenical engagement with the episcopally governed communions to which doctrines of ministry and episcopé are essential."); and David Preus ("Lutherans ought to be saying loudly and clearly that there is no deeper level of fellowship than to be in agreement in the Gospel, and as a result to be sharing in pulpit and altar fellowship. To accept 'full communion' language is to accept the notion that there is something more than agreement in the Gospel and administration of the sacraments that is necessary in order for Christians to reach the deepest

level of fellowship"). But appreciation for the term was also expressed. See especially the response of Bruce Marshall to an earlier draft: "At a number of points the Church's ecumenical mandate is traced to John 17, suggesting that the unity we seek is described in those passages. At some other points, the ecumenical task is characterized in terms of 'expressing'. . . or 'manifesting'. . . the unity of the church. This sort of language could be taken to mean that the church is already united in the sense of John 17, so that full communion, while desirable, can be absent without the loss of unity which Christ intends for and creates in the church. Read in this way, the document might give aid and comfort to the view. . .[that] there is no need to get worked up about bilateral dialogue, let alone about full communion, because believers are already united by faith in Christ. Appealing to a unity of faith in this way seems quite incompatible with John 17, in which a) the unity of the church must be apparent to the world, b) that visible unity is the primary and efficacious sign in and to the world of the supreme unity, that of the Father and the Son, and c) the only adequate analogue to the unity of the church is this inner-trinitarian unity of the Father and the Son, in which the church (precisely in its visibility: 'so that the world may know') participates."

4. See *Ways to Community* (Geneva: Lutheran World Federation, 1981), 25. "The goal of full communion towards which Catholic and Lutheran Christians and churches are now moving together points far beyond itself. It points to the perfect communion which we shall have with the Triune God at the end of time. But it also points beyond itself in the sense that Roman Catholic-Lutheran fellowship is not yet the fellowship of all Christians. We must see our rapprochement in the *context of the whole ecumenical movement* [emphasis in original], and not least in relationship to the notable institutional expression of that movement in the World Council of Churches."

5. *Ecumenical Perspective and Guidelines*, 11. Cf. Harding Meyer, "Models of Unity" in *Vision: oikoume* (Washington, D.C.: The Washington Institute of Ecumenics, 1986), 6: The church's unity, "which is a part of its very essence, is a gift because it is rooted in the one Lord. It is also a task because this unity must be made visible and effective in history."

6. *Niagara Report*, 61. Cf. response by Todd Nichol in *Responses to the Proposed Statement*, in which he cites the report as evidence that the term full communion has been identified as "problematic."

7. *Facing Unity: Models, Forms and Phases of Catholic-Lutheran Fellowship* (Geneva: Lutheran World Federation, 1985), 22-23.

8. Emphasis in original document. With regard to reception, see *Ways to Community* (Geneva: Lutheran World Federation, 1981), 2: "The reception of these results of the dialogue by our churches is an urgent task and step towards unity."

9. *Anglican-Lutheran Dialogue*, "The Report of the Anglican-Lutheran European Regional Commission, Helsinki, August-September (London: SPCK, 1982), 29.

10. *Facing Unity*, 36.

11. *Baptism, Eucharist and Ministry* [BEM], Faith and Order Paper no. 111 (Geneva: World Council of Churches, 1982), vii-viii.

12. Eugene Brand, *Toward A Lutheran Communion: Pulpit and Altar Fellowship,* LWF Report no. 26 (Geneva: Lutheran World Federation, 1988), 86.

13. See Harding Meyer, "Models of Unity," *Vision: oikoume,* vol. 3 (Washington, D.C.: Institute of Ecumenics, 1986), 6-11.

14. See *Ways to Community,* 14: "Our search is for steps in 'a process of gradual rapprochement. . . in which various stages are possible' ["Report of the Lutheran-Roman Catholic Study commission on 'The Gospel and the Church', 1972" ("Malta Report")]. In such an open process of growing together we can and should set our eyes on *intermediate goals* [emphasis in original] and keep on re-examining the methods of advance. By moving in this way from an incomplete to a more and more complete communion, we shall be able to take account of a wide variety of different historical, theological and regional situations. In being willing to enter into such an open process, we are well aware that God the Holy Spirit himself will show us steps and lead us in paths which for the most part we cannot at present envisage."

15. *Ways to Community,* VII.

16. *The Ministry in the Church* (Geneva: Lutheran World Federation, 1982), 31. See also 32: "The hope of achieving full church and eucharistic fellowship is not based on our human possibilities, but is rather founded on the promise of the Lord who through his Spirit is effectively manifest in the growing unity of our churches."

17. BEM, ix.

18. See note 17 above.

19. *Anglican-Lutheran Dialogue,* 29-31.

20. The commentary on the agreement at this point says (6): "The churches are not talking about structural union. They realize this agreement is one step, a first step, in faith together on a long road. They look forward to 'full communion' as a hope not a present reality. 'Full communion' or, more accurately expressed, 'intercommunion'–where two churches not of the same confessional family allow communicant members freely to communicate at the altar of each and where there is freedom of ministers to officiate sacramentally in either church–is not established by this agreement." Moreover, "this agreement does not foreclose any future option of Christian unity. . . . It does not describe any form of arrangements that would be in place for full communion, intercommunion, to be practiced."

21. *Facing Unity,* 23.

22. *Facing Unity,* 22.

23. *Facing Unity,* 31 n. 79. CA VII is invoked here. See also Günther Gassmann and Harding Meyer, *The Unity of the Church: Requirements and Structures.* LWF Report no. 15. (Geneva: Lutheran World Federation, 1983).

24. *Auf dem Weg zu sichtbarer Einheit* (Berlin: Evangelischen Kirchen in Der Deutschen Demokratischen Republik; Hannover: Evangelischen Kirche in Deutschland, 1988), 10-12.

25. *Auf dem Weg,* 20.

26. *Responses to the Proposed Statement,* a memorandum of 16 January 1989 by Todd Nichol. Cf. the response of 4 April 1989 of Luther Northwestern Theological Seminary: "In the context of the ecumenical discussion the fact that 'something more'

is taken to be necessary for full communion means that Lutheran ministry is defective and must be 'upgraded' by proper 'ordering' (episcopal succession, ordination and the like) before 'full communion' can be realized. The Lutheran doctrine of ministry is jeopardized. . . . The document states that 'full communion' can be attained only by an alteration in our ordering of episcopacy and ministry."

27. *Toward Church Fellowship* (Geneva: Lutheran World Federation, 1989).

28. *Toward Church Fellowship*, 28-29.

29. A memorandum from Todd Nichol dated 16 January 1989 in *Responses to the Proposed Statement*.

30. Brand, *Toward a Lutheran Communion*, 73. See Appendix II, Section G.

31. Brand, *Toward a Lutheran Communion*, 77-78. Here he cites Eric W. Gritsch and Robert W. Jenson, *Lutheranism* (Philadelphia: Fortress Press, 1976), 130. See Walter Kasper, "The Church as Communion," *Theology & Church* (London: SCM Press, 1989), 157. See also *Communio/Koinonia*, A Study by the Institute for Ecumenical Research (Geneva: Institute for Ecumenical Research, 1990; included as Appendix 2 in this volume).

32. Brand, *Toward a Lutheran Communion*, 82-83. He cites LC II. 47-53 and LW 35. 45ff. (WA 2. 742ff.) respectively.

33. Response of 13 January 1989 by Gerhard Forde in *Responses to the Proposed Statement*. Cf. the 20 February 1989 response by Lynn Lorenzen: "It was noted that Article VII of the Augsburg Confession may be applied as either a maximum of what is necessary for 'full communion' or as a minimum requirement for 'full communion' with other concerns decided on the basis of the partner communion."

34. See the *Sechstes Plenartreffen der Gemeinsamen Evangelisch-Lutherisch/Römisch-Katholischen Kommission*, 18-24 February 1980, 26. Cf. the complete text, 25-26: "If, as the Augsburg Confession (Art. VII) declares, agreement in these two marks is sufficient (*satis est*) for the true unity of the Church, this represents the fundamental condition for the affirmation of church unity. The '*satis*' should therefore not be misunderstood to mean that it would no longer be legitimate to affirm further agreements. If such further agreements are described as 'not necessary,' this is not only not intended to prevent the growth of unity in Christ, not even as regards the form of the Church but actually opens up the right way to such growth: as an expression of the gift in the Gospel, an expression that, like the works of the justified sinner, should follow this faith. Understood in this manner, the Lutheran "*satis est*" is therefore not opposed to the demand for the "fullness" of church life but actually opens up the way to this fullness. But, of course, this raises the question as to which form of church government would be most effective for the proclamation of the Gospel and for the life and mission of the Church." For example see Harding Meyer and Heinz Schütte, "The Concept of the Church in the Augustana Confession," *Confessing One Faith: A Joint Commentary on the Augsburg Confession by Lutheran and Catholic Theologians* (Minneapolis: Augsburg, 1982), 173-201.

35. "The Unity We Seek," *Budapest 1984: Proceedings of the Seventh Assembly*, LWF Report nos. 19/20 (Geneva: Lutheran World Federation, 1985), 175.

36. See Appendix 3.

# Concluding Comments

Official documents of churches often need to be terse. They have little opportunity to root their ideas and positions in the larger sweep of history or in the consensus of earlier teaching by means of extensive texts and lengthy footnotes. This characteristic of brevity and directness is not only understandable but advantageous in view of the use of such statements within a church. Official texts should not be tomes. The drafters of *Ecumenism: The Vision of the Evangelical Lutheran Church in America* have endeavored to respect the genus of the document.

*Ecumenism: The Vision of the Evangelical Lutheran Church in America* is a significant text not merely for the church that adopted it as a working document in 1989, but for many ecumenical partners in this country and elsewhere. Its ideas and suggestions for ecumenical advance have occasioned wholesome discussion and a reexamination of the fundamental commitments of confessional Lutheranism within the ELCA. To inform and assist this reflection, a volume was required that would offer a more detailed review of the main features of the text of *Ecumenism* and place them in a broad Lutheran and ecumenical context.

Any commentary on the statement could be more exhaustive, and the documentation could be fuller than that given in the previous pages. Those who have developed this book are convinced that even with the limitations of time and resources available to produce this commentary, it addresses the major questions that have been asked of *Ecumenism: The Vision of the Evangelical Lutheran Church in America*. The intention of this commentary is to supply documentation that places *Ecumenism* within the mainstream of Lutheran and ecumenical theology.

The commentary desires to show how *Ecumenism* is an adequate and responsible expression of Lutheran commitment to the ecumenical movement. Only as individual readers work through the document and the illustrative commentary will they be able to judge the extent to which this claim is justified. These pages are offered in the spirit of promoting helpful theological reflection about one of the major areas of work of the ELCA, or of any church – that of furthering under God's Spirit the unity of Christ's people.

*Appendix* **1**

# The Relation Between
# Satis Est *and*
# Full Communion

## An Opinion from the Institute for
## Ecumenical Research, Strasbourg

1. The *satis est* clause of the Augsburg Confession (7.2) describes that which suffices for the true unity of the church: When churches *agree* (are in *consensus*) in the *pure preaching of the gospel* and the *evangelical administration of the sacraments*, then the true unity of the church is present. It is not necessary for the true unity of the Church that "traditions, rites, and ceremonies, instituted by men, should be alike everywhere" (7.3).

> The Augsburg Confession, Article 7.2, states: "For the true unity [*veram unitatem, wahrer Einigkeit*] of the church it is enough [*satis est, Dies ist gnug*] to agree [*consentire, einträchtiglich*] concerning the teaching of the Gospel and the administration of the sacraments." The German version adds that the agreement must concern the Gospel "preached in conformity with a pure understanding of it" and the sacraments "administered in accordance with the divine Word."[1] Two aspects of this clause need here to be noted.
>
> First, the *satis est* clause refers to an agreement, consensus, or harmony in the preaching of the Gospel and administration of the sacraments. The standard English translation of the German version of CA obscures the importance of agreement by failing to give any equivalent for the German word *einträchtiglich*, i.e., harmoniously, in agreement, or in concord. In the context of the discussions at Augsburg, "agreement" or "concord" is best interpreted as referring to an agreement in some way explicitly realized and not the mere objective presence of the same teaching or sacraments in two churches.
>
> Second, *satis est* describes that which *suffices* for the true unity of the church. This particular formulation is rooted in the situation CA addressed. At Augsburg, the question needed to be answered: Had the evangelical estates

either left or broken the unity of the church by the changes introduced in the preaching and practices of their churches? CA insists that the Lutherans have in no way left or broken the true unity of the church. Part 1 as a whole is meant to demonstrate that the Lutheran teaching "is not contrary or opposed to that of the universal Christian church or even of the Roman church (insofar as the latter's teaching is reflected in the writings of the Fathers)" (CA, Conclusion of Part I, 1). Within this wider argument, *satis est* gives greater specificity to the argument that the Lutherans have not left or broken the unity of the church by describing the elements that create that unity. For true unity, consensus in pure preaching and rightly administered sacraments suffices. If the Lutherans have not abandoned the agreement of "the universal Christian church" on these matters, then they have not left or broken the true unity of the church. This is the apologetic intention of *satis est*.[2]

This apologetic intention explains why CA 7 explicitly states only that these elements are *sufficient* for the unity of the church. It does not explicitly state that they are *necessary* for unity, though that may be implied by the total article. This necessity is not explicitly mentioned because it was not there and then disputed. The question was whether these elements sufficed for true unity.[3]

**1.1.** *Satis est* must be interpreted in the textual context of the entire CA and the historical context of the Reformation and the Diet of Augsburg.

*Satis est* is one sentence in a much larger document. It must not be isolated from the remainder of CA but interpreted as a part of CA. Most notably, it must be interpreted in relation to CA's total ecclesiology. For example, *satis est* must not be isolated from the assertion of the divine institution of the office of ministry in CA 5. The exact interpretation of the interrelation *satis est* and CA 5 is not decisive for what we say here and is briefly addressed below under "*Satis est* and the Divinely Instituted Office of Ministry." It should be remembered, however, that agreement on the right preaching of the gospel and right administration of the sacraments will include agreement on whatever they may presuppose about the office of ministry.

Any interpretation of *satis est* must also note the historical context of CA. CA was written within a Western church experiencing great tensions, but still widely believed to be one church.[4] CA at places simply assumes certain common structures (e.g., a common ordained ministry in Arts. 14 and 28). At other places, it directly appeals to other possible institutions (e.g., a universal council, Preface 21) that might serve the unity of the church and help bring about the consensus referred to in *satis est*. *Satis est* must not be isolated from the institutions which the Reformers assumed as part of the life of the church.

**1.2.** In its rejection of "human traditions" as "necessary for the true unity of the church," *satis est* rejects these traditions as "necessary for righteousness before God" and thus expresses the doctrine of justification by faith alone.

For the Reformers, the question of what is necessary for justification and what is necessary for the true unity of the Church were closely interwoven. The Apology says in its interpretation of *satis est*: "With a very thankful spirit we cherish the useful and ancient ordinances. . . . Now, we are not discussing whether it is profitable to observe them for the sake of tranquility or bodily profit. Another issue is involved. The question is whether the observance of human traditions is an act of worship necessary for righteousness before God. This must be settled in this controversy, and only then can we decide whether it is necessary for the true unity of the church that human traditions be alike everywhere" (Apol. 7.33f). In this way, *satis est* brings the doctrine of justification by grace through faith to bear on ecclesiology. Only agreement in those divinely instituted means of grace which communicate free justification is *in the strict sense* necessary to the true unity of the church. As this quotation shows, such an assertion in no way denies that beside these divinely instituted means of grace that are necessary both for righteousness before God and for the true unity of the church, there are also rites, ordinances, and structures which are good, useful, and beneficial to the concrete realization of unity. These traditions can be "cherished" with a "thankful spirit."[5]

**1.3.** The unity described in *satis est* is the "true unity of the church."

*Satis est* itself calls the unity it describes the "true unity of the church." It is not some preliminary or provisional unity. When churches are one in the sense of *satis est*, no additional elements can be considered essential to the true unity of the church, as is explicitly stated in CA 7.3.

**2.** *Full communion* refers to the same unity as *satis est*, but spells it out in terms of a set of relations among churches.

*Full communion* refers to a set of relations among churches through which they seek to live out or realize their unity in Christ as described in *satis est* (see note 6, §5).[6] These relations might be among churches in the sense of denominations, or among congregations or dioceses within a larger church body.

**2.1.** One can find in recent ecumenical documents a consensus that *full communion* involves at least four elements: (1) unity in the confession of the faith, the preaching of the gospel, and the administration of the sacraments, (2) mutual acceptability of members and ordained ministers, (3) some forms of common life and witness and related structures for consultation and common decision making, and (4) the lifting of any relevant past doctrinal condemnations.

Appendix 3 shows how the explicit meaning of *full communion* has expanded since the attempt to define ecumenical terms at the 1952 World Conference on Faith and Order at Lund (App. 3, §17). If one focuses on the most recent statements, a broad consensus on the meaning of *full communion* emerges (see, e.g., the Lutheran-Reformed report *Toward Church Fellowship* [App. 3, §6], the Lutheran-Anglican *Cold Ash Report* [App. 3, §8], the UCC-Disciples of Christ *Vision Statement* [App. 3, §11], the Bangalore Faith and Order Statement [App. 3, §22]), the LWF statement on "The Unity We Seek" [App. 3, §17], and the Anglican *Emmaus Report* [App. 3, §24]). *Full communion* implies more than declarations of mutual acceptability. It involves at least four elements listed in the thesis. Succinctly, to say that the goal of ecumenical work is *full communion* is to say that the goal is more than mutual openness, but also includes a genuine common life and the forms of common decision making such a common life requires.

The last element on the list, the lifting of relevant past doctrinal condemnations, is found in ecumenical documents with less frequency than the other elements. Among many Protestant churches, there are in fact no relevant past doctrinal condemnations. Where such condemnations exist, their remaining validity is incompatible with "true unity" and their lifting must be an element of *full communion*. The Leuenberg Agreement of 1973, perhaps the best known example of Lutheran churches entering into a relationship of *full communion* or fellowship with non-Lutheran churches, involved the mutual lifting of condemnations (§§20, 23, 26-28). The mutual lifting of condemnations between Lutherans and Roman Catholics has been extensively discussed in Germany and is addressed in the most recent international Lutheran-Roman Catholic dialogue statement.[7]

To describe these four elements is not to state what are the conditions of their attainment. Here, churches disagree. For example, an Orthodox would say that a precondition for the "mutual acceptability of ordained ministers" is that all ministers be ordained by bishops in historical succession. A Presbyterian would reject such a claim. They might still agree, however, that an essential aspect of *full communion* is the mutual acceptability of ordained ministers. It should be noted that *full communion* in no way implies the necessity or advisability of any particular ordering of episcopé.

**2.2.** *Full communion* as defined in the ELCA Ecumenism statement is in accord with the accepted use of the term in ecumenical documents.

This agreement is immediately clear from a comparison of the statement, section II.D, and the previous thesis.

**2.3.** If there is an area of controversy in the meaning of *full communion*, it would be in relation to structures for consultation and common decision making.

The need for structures of common decision making has become a standard ingredient in the understanding of *full communion*. Nevertheless, just what form such common decision making should take remains controversial. To a degree, these structures cannot be defined in the abstract, since they will vary from relation to relation. The sort of common life and witness and related decision making the ELCA might appropriately realize with the Presbyterian Church (USA) would be significantly different from that realized with the Presbyterian Church in, say, Ghana. At the very least, common actions will require forms of common decision making in relation to such common actions. The open question is: If no Christian community is the Church in isolation from the rest of the Church, to what degree should decisions about fundamental matters be made independently and to what degree in relation to other communities? There is no agreed answer to this question as yet. The concept of *full communion* only suggests the general principle that life together implies some forms of common decision making.

**3.** The unity referred to in *satis est* is itself communion in Christ and thus communion with each other.

While CA 7 does not itself use the term "communion" to describe the church or its unity, Melanchthon's interpretation of this article in the *Apology* does. The phrase used to define the church in CA 7.1, the "assembly of all believers," is explicitly identified by Melanchthon with the "communion of saints" confessed in the Apostles' Creed (Apol. 7:8). For Luther also, the church is a *communio* (Lg. Cat., II:48f). The unity of the church is rooted in our participation or communion in the one Christ who comes to us in the pure preaching of the gospel and the evangelically administered sacraments. As we commonly participate in Christ through the Word preached and sacraments celebrated, we are one with each other. The unity of the church is thus grounded in a common communion in Christ.[8]

**4.** The unity of the church described by *satis est* is inseparable from a lived communion among churches.

*Satis est* must not be interpreted as reducing the unity of the church to a static common possession of certain elements. Unity is not rightly realized by mere mutual tolerance. First, *satis est* sees the unity of the church in its coming together in a consensus or unanimity on Word and sacrament. This consensus requires a common agreement on all that is presupposed by the pure preaching of the gospel and the evangelical administration of the sacraments, e.g., on questions of ministry. The common life and witness in which the church lives out its unity is first and foremost a common life and witness in the preaching of the Word and celebration of the sacraments.

Second, it would misrepresent *satis est* and isolate it from the total ecclesiology and theology of the Reformation to fail to see that this unity in Word and sacrament has within it an impulse to a wider common life. Speaking of our fellowship or communion [*Gemeinschaft*] in the Lord's Supper, Luther says: "This fellowship is twofold: on the one hand we partake of Christ and all saints; on the other hand we permit all Christians to be partakers of us, in whatever way they and we are able."[9] Similar statements can be found throughout Lutheran history. For example, the American Lutheran Conference's 1952 *United Testimony on Faith and Life* states: "Christian faith *seeks* fellowship, that is, the discovery and the practice of this spiritual fellowship with other Christians. It laments isolation; it yearns for communion. Christian faith seeks fellowship in prayer, in corporate worship, in Communion, in doing the Lord's work, and even in suffering for the faith."[10]

The unity described in *satis est* is itself a lived communion in Word and sacrament and contains within it an impulse to wider forms of common life and witness.

**5.** *Full communion* makes explicit those relations among churches through which they realize and live out the unity described in *satis est*.

*Satis est* gives a rather general statement of those elements which suffice for the true unity of the church. No additional elements can be required as essential to the church's unity. *Full communion* spells out in greater detail the relations between churches in which the unity described in *satis est* is concretely lived out. The realization and living out of a consensus on the preaching of the Word and celebration of the sacraments is itself a unity in the confession of the faith, the preaching of the gospel, and the administration of the sacraments as well as a form of common life and witness. The development and preservation of such a consensus require some structures, however simple, for consultation and common decision making. This unity in Word and sacrament must imply a mutual openness to each other's members and ordained ministers of Word and sacrament and would be incompatible with the continued applicability of past doctrinal condemnations. *Full communion* is thus best understood as making explicit what it means for churches to live out the unity described in *satis est*. Within *full communion*, churches will also seek ways to realize the wider common life and witness toward which we are impelled by the unity described in *satis est*. To say that a church's ecumenical goal is *full communion* is to say that it seeks to realize and live out the unity described in *satis est* in its relations with other churches.

Appendix 2 shows both that *full communion* has become a widely used phrase to describe the goal of ecumenical work and that it is generally used to describe the realization and living out of the unity of the church. "Communion" or "fellowship" as the living out of unity has been important in the development of Lutheran ecumenism in the postwar period.[11] Papers presented to the Theology Commission of the LWF in the 1950s on the theme of church unity developed this idea with particular force.[12]

These earlier Lutheran discussions form the background for the important ecumenical statements from the 1984 Assembly of the LWF (App. 2, §§17, 18). In its statement on "The Unity We Seek," reference is initially made to "the true unity of the church, which is the unity of the body of Christ and . . . is given in and through proclamation of the gospel in Word and sacrament." The phrase "true unity" here echoes CA 7. This statement is immediately followed by the assertion: "This unity is expressed as a communion," a communion which is then described in terms which spell out the four commonly cited elements of *full communion* noted above. Similarly, in the statement on "The Self- Understanding and Task of the LWF" the sorts of relations described by *full communion* are called a "visible expression" of the unity of the Lutheran churches. For both statements, unity as described in *satis est* is realized and lived out in relations of *full communion*.

**6.** *Full communion* as ecumenical goal in no way contradicts *satis est*.

As should be clear from the analysis developed, we see no contradiction between *satis est* and *full communion*. On the contrary, to attempt to realize the unity described in *satis est* without relations of full communion is to live in self-contradiction.

**6.1.** *Satis est* and *full communion* would be in contradiction *if full communion* described as necessary for the true unity of the church elements beyond those included in, implied by or required for the realization of *satis est*, which is not the case.

What would need to be the case for *full communion* and *satis est* to stand in contradiction? *Full communion* would contradict *satis est* if it specified elements beyond those included in, implied by or required for *satis est* as essential to the unity of the church. As is clear from our discussion above (5), *full communion* does not do so.

**6.2.** *Satis est* and *full communion* would be in contradiction *if full communion* implied that the unity referred to in *satis est* were not the "true unity of the church," which is not the case.

*Satis est* describes the "true unity of the church." This unity is realized and lived out in the concrete lives of the churches more or less "fully." The unity given in the elements of *satis est* is nevertheless complete. Similar statements can be said about the Christian's unity with Christ in faith. Faith unites us fully with Christ. This faith is realized and lived out in a life of faith, which testifies to and realizes faith within the everyday more or less fully. This "more or less fully" does not call into question the fullness of unity with Christ in faith.

**6.3.** *Satis est* and *full communion* would be in contradiction if the relations referred to by *full communion* were somehow incompatible with consensus in the pure preaching of the gospel and evangelical administration of the sacraments, which is not the case.

To demonstrate such an incompatibility one would have to show how at least one of the elements of *full communion* referred to above (2.1) *in itself* undermined consensus in true preaching and evangelical sacraments. Of course a false united confession of faith or perhaps a triumphalistic structure of common decision making might be incompatible with the true preaching of the gospel. But such possibilities do not imply that the elements of *full communion* in themselves, as such, are incompatible with *satis est*. We see no way such an incompatibility could be plausibly asserted.

7. The communion realized in *full communion* is full in the sense that it seeks to create a structure adequate to the historical living out of unity, though we know that within that structure we will often fail fully to live out our oneness in Christ.

> *Full communion* is not the realization of perfect unity within history. Perfect unity with each other and with Christ will only come eschatologically. Rather, *full communion* refers to the relations among churches which can be judged to be adequate to our attempts here and now to live out our unity. When churches are in *full communion*, their failures to live out communion are not then a function of the presence or absence of the relations referred to by *full communion*, but of how well or poorly within these relations we are "united in love without sect or schism" (Lg. Cat., II.51).

## SATIS EST AND THE
## DIVINELY INSTITUTED OFFICE OF MINISTRY

The assertion in CA 5 that "God instituted the office of ministry" can raise the question whether it belongs to the pure preaching of the gospel and right administration of the sacraments that they be carried out by the office of ministry. Our opinion of the relation between *satis est* and *full communion* does not depend on any particular answer to this question and so no extensive discussion of the interrelation of CA 5 and CA 7 is here offered. Some brief comments, however, can be offered as an appendix to our opinion.

On the one hand, a consistent reading of CA would require that CA 7.2 and 5.1 be read as consistent with each other. Such a reading would require that the right preaching of the gospel and celebration of the sacraments somehow presupposes the office of ministry. On the other hand, it is not insignificant that the office of ministry is not explicitly mentioned in 7.2. Whatever significance the office of ministry has for the existent and unity of the church, the office is subordinate to the Word and sacraments which constitute the church and its unity.[13]

How the interrelation between CA 7 and 5 is worked out will make some difference for the place of the mutual recognition of ordained ministries in discussions between churches. On the one hand, if one judges that CA 7 presupposes the office of ministry as a condition for pure preaching and evangelical sacraments, then recognition of ministries will be a necessary element in the recognition of true oneness with another church. On the other hand, if one judges that CA 7 does not presuppose CA 5 in this way, then the mutual recognition of ministries will instead be a moment in the development of common forms of life and witness that follows from the recognition of unity. Differing ways of interrelating CA 5 and CA 7 will determine the place of the mutual recognition of ordained ministries in the ecumenical process, but they do not affect the opinion offered here on the interrelation of *satis est* and *full communion*.

## NOTES

1. Translation in *The Book of Concord: The Confessions of the Evangelical Lutheran Church*, ed. Theodore G. Tappert (Philadelphia: Fortress Press, 1959), 32.

2. See Bernhard Lohse, "Die Einheit der Kirche," 65, 72, 79; and W. Maurer, *Historical Commentary*, 379; but also Ernst Kinder, "Basic Considerations with Reference to Article VII," *Unity of the Church: A Symposium* (Rock Island, IL: Augustana Press, 1957), 59; R. Schultz, "Article VII.2," 26, 30; and H. Sasse, "Article VII," 44.

3. On the necessity of these elements, see E. Schlink, "Kriterien der Einheit," 112.

4. See B. Lohse, 59f; E. Kinder, 59f.

5. See Harding Meyer and Heinz Schütte, "The Concept of the Church in the Augustana Confession," *Confessing One Faith: A Joint Commentary on the Augsburg Confession by Lutheran and Catholic Theologians* (Minneapolis: Augsburg, 1982), 184-88.

6. A problem in tracing the use of the phrase full communion in ecumenical texts is the translation into English of the German term *Kirchengemeinschaft*. *Gemeinschaft* can be translated "fellowship," "community," or, especially in theological contexts, "communion." The standard French translation of *Kirchengemeinschaft* is *communion ecclesiale*. The texts from the 1984 Budapest Assembly of the LWF consistently use the German "Gemeinschaft" and the English "communion" as equivalent. The English "fellowship" is also used, but only sparingly. The translators of the international Lutheran/Catholic dialogue texts have tended to use "communion" when a technical sense is implied, especially if the Latin term "communio" seems to be in the background, and "fellowship" at other times. Compare the English and German especially of *Facing Unity/Einheit vor Uns*, §5f. The German version of the Lund 1952 definitions of ecumenical terms translates *full communion* as *volle Abendmahlsgemeinschaft*. While English texts of the Leuenberg Agreement usually translate *Kirchengemeinschaft* as "church fellowship," the later Lutheran-Reformed statement *Toward Church Fellowship*, §29, explicitly describes the Leuenberg Agreement as a declaration of *full communion*. We will here assume that in the context of the discussion of church relations, "church fellowship" and "communion" refer to the same set of relations and that each is the English equivalent to *Kirchengemeinschaft* and to *communion ecclesiale*. On these translation difficulties, see Brand, *Toward Lutheran Communion*, 12f.

7. For the German discussion, see Lehmann and Pannenberg, *The Condemnations of the Reformation Era*. For the dialogue statement, see *Facing Unity*, §§67-69.

8. See *Communio/Koinonia: A New Testament-Early Christian Concept and its Contemporary Appropriation and Significance*. A Study by the Institute for Ecumenical Research, Strasbourg (Strasbourg: 1990), 15f.

9. "The Blessed Sacrament of the Holy and True Body of Christ, and the Brotherhoods," *Luther's Works*, American Edition, vol. 35, 67 (Weimar Ausgabe, vol. 2, 754).

10. Wolf, *Documents of Lutheran Unity in America*, 510. The 1970 Lutheran-Reformed Leuenberg Report, forerunner of the Leuenberg Agreement, strikes a similar note: "This spiritual communion or fellowship impels [*drängt*] us toward the greatest possible cooperation [*Gemeinsamkeit*] in inner church life and in witness and service in the world." In E. Scheiffer, *Von Schauenburg nach Leuenberg: Entstehung und Bedeutung der Konkordie reformatorischer Kirchen in Europa*. Paderborn: Verlag Bonifatius-Druckerei, 1983.

11. See H. Meyer, "Zur Entstehung und Bedeutung des Konzepts 'Kirchengemeinschaft.' "

12. Some of these essays are collected in *The Unity of the Church: A Symposium*. Papers presented to the Commission on Theology and Liturgy of the Lutheran World Federation.

13. On these questions, see Edmund Schlink, *Theology of the Lutheran Confessions*, 202; and H. Meyer & H. Schütte, "The Concept of the Church," 187f.

## APPENDIX 1 BIBLIOGRAPHY

Anglican Ecumenical Consultation. *The Emmaus Report*. A report of the Anglican Ecumenical Consultation that took place at the Emmaus Retreat Centre, West Wickham, Kent, England, 27 January-2 February 1987 in preparation for ACC-7, Singapore, 1987 and The Lambeth Conference, 1988. London: Anglican Consultative Council, 1987.

Anglican-Lutheran European Commission. *Anglican-Lutheran Dialogue: Helsinki Report 1982*. London: SPCK, 1983.

Anglican-Lutheran Joint Working Group. *Anglican-Lutheran Relations: The Cold Ash Report*. London: Anglican Consultative Council; Geneva: Lutheran World Federation, 1983.

*Anglican-Orthodox Dialogue: The Dublin Agreed Statement 1984*. London: SPCK, 1984.

*Auf dem Weg zu sichtbarer Einheit. Eine gemeinsame Feststellung/On the Way to Visible Unity: A Common Statement*. Berlin and Hannover: 1988.

"*Beyond Intercommunion: On the Way to Communion in the Eucharist*. A study paper of the Commission on Faith and Order." *Study Encounter* 5 (1969):94-114.

Bornkamm, Heinrich. "Die Kirche in der Confessio Augustana." In *Das Jahrhundert der Reformation: Gestalten und Kräfte*, 133-41. Göttingen: Vandenhoeck & Ruprecht, 1961.

Bornkamm, Heinrich. *Luther in Mid-Career 1521-1530.* Edited by Karin Bornkamm. Translated by E. Theodore Bachmann. Philadelphia: Fortress Press, 1983.

Braaten, Carl E. *Principles of Lutheran Theology.* Philadelphia: Fortress Press, 1983.

Brand, Eugene L. *Toward a Lutheran Communion: Pulpit and Altar Fellowship.* LWF Report no. 26. Geneva: Lutheran World Federation, 1988.

Brunner, Peter. "The Realization of Church Fellowship." In *The Unity of the Church: A Symposium*, Papers presented to the Commission on Theology and Liturgy of the Lutheran World Federation, 11-22. Rock Island, Illinois: Augustana Press, 1957.

*Budapest 1984: "In Christ—Hope for the World."* Official Proceedings of the Seventh Assembly of the Lutheran World Federation. LWF Report nos. 19/20 (1985).

Cooper, Charles W., Jr. "New Ecumenical Partnership of The United Church of Christ and Disciples of Christ." *Ecumenical Trends* 17 (1988):113-15.

Decree on Ecumenism, *Unitatis Redintegratio.* In *The Documents of Vatican II*, edited by Walter M. Abbott, 336-70. N.p. Geoffrey Chapman, 1966.

Elert, Werner. *The Structure of Lutheranism.* Vol. 1., *The Theology and Philosophy of Life of Lutheranism Especially in the Sixteenth and Seventeenth Centuries.* Translated by Walter A. Hansen. St. Louis: Concordia Publishing House, 1962.

Faith and Order Commission, World Council of Churches. *Bangalore 1978: Sharing in One Hope.* Reports and Documents from the Meeting of the Faith and Order Commission, 15-30 August 1978, Bangalore, India. Geneva: World Council of Churches, 1978.

Fraenkel, Pierre. "Satis Est? Schrift, Tradition, Bekenntnis," in *Confessio Augustana und Confutatio: Der Augsburger Reichstag 1530 und die Einheit der Kirche.* Reformationsgeschichtliche Studien und Texte, 118. Edited by Erwin Iserloh, 286-300. Münster: Aschendorff, 1980.

Grane, Leif. *The Augsburg Confession: A Commentary.* Translated by John H. Rasmussen. Minneapolis: Augsburg, 1987.

Gritsch, Eric W., and Robert W. Jenson. *Lutheranism: The Theological Movement and Its Confessional Writings.* Philadelphia: Fortress Press, 1976.

*An Invitation to Action: A Study of Ministry, Sacraments, and Recognition. The Lutheran-Reformed Dialogue Series III, 1981-1983.* Edited by James E. Andrews and Joseph A. Burgess. Philadelphia: Fortress Press, 1984.

Jenson, Robert W. "Lutheran Conditions for Communion in Holy Things." In *Lutheran-Episcopal Dialogue: A Progress Report*, 127-38. Cincinnati: Forward Movement Publications, 1973.

Joint Commission between the Roman Catholic Church and the World Methodist Council. "Towards a Statement on the Church: Report of the Joint Commission between the Roman Catholic Church and the World Methodist Council, 1982-1986 (Fourth Series)." *One In Christ* 22 (1986):241-59.

Kandler, Karl-Hermann. "CA VII—Konzentration und Weite lutherischer Ekklesiologie." *Kerygma und Dogma* 35 (1989):70-83.

Kasper, Walter. "Kirchenverständnis und Kircheneinheit nach der Confessio Augustana," in *Evangelium – Sakramente – Amt und die Einheit der Kirche: Die ökumenische Tragweite der Confessio Augustana*, edited by Karl Lehmann and Edmund Schlink, Dialog der Kirchen, 2, 28-57. Freiburg i. B.: Herder; Göttingen: Vandenhoeck & Ruprecht, 1982.

Kinder, Ernst. "Basic Considerations with reference to Article VII of the Augsburg Confession." In *The Unity of the Church: A Symposium*, Papers presented to the Commission on Theology and Liturgy of the Lutheran World Federation, 59-73. Rock Island, Illinois: Augustana Press, 1957.

*Lambeth Conference 1968: Resolutions and Reports*. London: SPCK; New York: Seabury, 1968.

Lehmann, Karl, and Wolfhart Pannenberg, eds. *The Condemnations of the Reformation Era: Do They Still Divide?* Minneapolis: Fortress Press, 1989.

Lohse, Bernhard. "Die Einheit der Kirche nach der Confessio Augustana." In *Evangelium – Sakramente – Amt und die Einheit der Kirche: Die ökumenische Tragweite der Confessio Augustana*. Edited by Karl Lehmann and Edmund Schlink, Dialog der Kirchen, 2, 58-79. Freiburg i. B.: Herder; Göttingen: Vandenhoeck & Ruprecht, 1982.

Luther, Martin. "The Blessed Sacrament of the Holy and True Body of Christ, and the Brotherhoods." Translated by Jeremiah Schindel, revised by E. Theodore Bachmann. In *Luther's Works*, vol. 35, *Word and Sacrament*, I, 45-73. Philadelphia: Fortress Press, 1960.

——. *Confession Concerning Christ's Supper*. Translated by Robert H. Fischer. In *Luther's Works*, vol. 37, *Word and Sacrament*, III, 151-372. Philadelphia: Fortress Press, 1961.

——. *On the Councils and the Church*. Translated by Charles M. Jacobs, revised by Eric W. Gritsch. In *Luther's Works*, vol. 41, *Church and Ministry*, III, 3-178. Philadelphia: Fortress Press, 1966.

——. *On the Papacy in Rome, Against the Most Celebrated Romanist in Leipzig*. Translated by Eric W. Gritsch and Ruth C. Gritsch. In *Luther's Works*, vol. 39, *Church and Ministry*, I, 49-104. Philadelphia: Fortress Press, 1970.

*Lutheran-Episcopal Agreement: Commentary and Guidelines*. New York: Division for World Mission and Ecumenism, Lutheran Church in America, 1983.

Lutheran-Reformed Joint Commission. *Toward Church Fellowship*. Geneva: Lutheran World Federation and World Alliance of Reformed Churches, 1989.

Martensen, Daniel F. *The Federation and the World Council of Churches*. LWF Report no. 3. Geneva: Lutheran World Federation, 1978.

Maurer, Wilhelm. *Historical Commentary on the Augsburg Confession*. Translated by H. George Anderson. Philadelphia: Fortress Press, 1986.

Meyer, Harding. *Evangelisches Staatslexikon*, 3rd ed., s.v., "Kirchengemeinschaft."

Meyer, Harding. "Roman Catholic/Lutheran Dialogue." *One in Christ*, 22 (1986): 146-68.

Meyer, Harding. "Zur Entstehung und Bedeutung des Konzepts 'Kirchengemeinschaft': Eine historische Skizze aus evangelischer Sicht." In *Communio Sanctorum: Einheit der Christen—Einheit der Kirche*, FS P.-W. Scheele. Edited by Josef Schreiner and Klaus Wittstadt, 204-30. Würzburg: Echter, 1988.

Meyer, Harding and Heinz Schütte. "The Concept of the Church in the Augsburg Confession." Translated by James L. Schaaf, in *Confessing One Faith: A Joint Commentary on the Augsburg Confession by Lutheran and Catholic Theologians*. Edited by George Wolfgang Forell and James F. McCue, 173-201. Minneapolis: Augsburg, 1982.

Meyer, Harding and Lukas Vischer, eds. *Growth in Agreement: Reports and Agreed Statements of Ecumenical Conversations on a World Level*. New York: Paulist Press; Geneva: World Council of Churches, 1984.

Oekumenischer Arbeitskreis evangelischer und katholischer Theologen. "Gemeinsame Erklärung: Zeichen der Einheit der Kirche in Anschluss an die Confessio Augustana: Evangelium—Sakramente—Amt," in *Evangelium—Sakramente—Amt und die Einheit der Kirche: Die ökumenische Tragweite der Confessio Augustana*. Edited by Karl Lehmann and Edmund Schlink, Dialog der Kirchen, 2, 184-90. Freiburg i. B.: Herder; Göttingen: Vandenhoeck & Ruprecht, 1982.

Oekumenischer Ausschuss der Vereinigten Evangelisch-Lutherischen Kirche Deutschlands. *Koinonia: Arbeiten des Oekumenischen Ausschusses der Vereinigten Evangelisch-Lutherischen Kirche Deutschlands zur Frage der Kirchen und Abendmahlsgemeinschaft*. Berlin: Lutherisches Verlagshaus, 1957.

Roman Catholic/Lutheran Joint Commission. *Facing Unity: Models, Forms and Phases of Catholic-Lutheran Church Fellowship*. Geneva: Lutheran World Federation, 1985.

———. *The Ministry in the Church*. Geneva: Lutheran World Federation, 1982.

———. *Ways to Community*. Geneva: Lutheran World Federation, 1981.

Sasse, Hermann. "Article VII of the Augsburg Confession in the Present Crisis of Lutheranism." In *We Confess the Church*. Translated by Norman Nagel, 40-68.

Schieffer, Elisabeth. *Von Schauenburg nach Leuenberg: Entstehung und Bedeutung der Konkordie reformatorischer Kirchen in Europa*. Konfessionskundliche und Kontroverstheologische Studien, 48. Paderborn: Bonifatius, 1983.

Schlink, Edmund. "Kriterien der Einheit der Kirche aufgrund der Augsburgischen Konfession," in *Evangelium—Sakramente—Amt und die Einheit der Kirche: Die ökumenische Tragweite der Confessio Augustana*. Edited by Karl Lehmann and Edmund Schlink, Dialog der Kirchen, 2, 109-121. Freiburg i. B.: Herder; Göttingen: Vandenhoeck & Ruprecht, 1982.

———. *Theology of the Lutheran Confessions*. Translated by Paul F. Koehneke and Herbert J. A. Bouman. Philadelphia: Fortress Press, 1961.

———. "Die Weite der Kirche nach dem lutherischen Bekenntnis." In *Der kommende Christus und die kirchlichen Traditionen: Beiträge zum Gespräch zwischen den getrennten Kirchen*, 106-15. Göttingen: Vandenhoeck & Ruprecht, 1961.

Schultz, Robert C. "An Analysis of the Augsburg Confession Article VII, 2, in its Historical Context, May & June, 1530." *Sixteenth Century Journal* 11 (1980): 25-35.

Teinonen, Seppo A. "Satis est—Augustana VII." In *Leuenberg—Konkordie oder Diskordie: Oekumenische Kritik zur Konkordie reformatorischer Kirchen in Europa*. Edited by Ulrich Asendorf & Friedrich Wilhelm Künneth, 155-63. Berlin & Schleswig-Holstein: Verlag Die Spur, 1974.

*The Three Reports of the Forum on Bilateral Conversations*. Faith and Order Paper no. 107. Geneva: World Council of Churches, 1981.

*The Unity of the Church: A Symposium*. Papers presented to the Commission on Theology and Liturgy of the Lutheran World Federation. Rock Island, Illinois: Augustana Press, 1957.

Vajta, Vilmos, ed. *Church in Fellowship: Pulpit and Altar Fellowship Among Lutherans*. Minneapolis: Augsburg, 1963.

———. "The Unity of the Church and Holy Communion." In *Church in Fellowship: Pulpit and Altar Fellowship Among Lutherans*, 222-72. Minneapolis: Augsburg, 1963.

Vischer, Lukas. ". . . satis est? Gemeinschaft in Christus und Einheit der Kirche." In *Christliche Freiheit—im Dienst am Menschen*, FS M. Niemöller. Edited by Karl Herbert, 243-54. Frankfurt: Verlag Otto Lembeck, 1972.

———, ed. *A Documentary History of the Faith and Order Movement 1927-1963*. St. Louis: Bethany Press, 1963.

Wiedenhofer, Siegfried. "Satis Est? Schrift, Tradition, Bekenntnis (Korreferat)." In *Confessio Augustana und Confutatio: Der Augsburger Reichstag 1530 und die Einheit der Kirche*. Reformationsgeschichtliche Studien und Texte, 118. Edited by Erwin Iserloh, 301-305. Münster: Aschendorff, 1980.

Wolf, Richard C. *Documents of Lutheran Unity in America*. Philadelphia: Fortress Press, 1966.

*Appendix* **2**

# Communio/Koinonia: A New Testament-Early Christian Concept and Its Contemporary Appropriation and Significance

## A Study by the Institute for Ecumenical Research, Strasbourg (1990)

### FOREWORD

*André Birmelé, Eugene L. Brand, Flemming Fleinert-Jensen, Harding Meyer, Michael Root, Yacob Tesfai*

For over a decade, the self-understanding and task of the Lutheran World Federation (LWF) have been intensely debated. The LWF Assembly in Budapest (1984) made important clarifications but did not end the discussion. As the LWF has considered restructuring, new aspects of the question have been opened up, and the question has taken on a new urgency.

The concept of communion (**communio/koinonia**) has been a focus for discussion at least since Budapest. This study of the meaning, historical background, and present use of the concept is offered by the Strasbourg Institute for Ecumenical Research as a contribution to these discussions.

This study has three chapters:

> The **first chapter** can be called the basic text. It attempts to outline the essential elements for an understanding of **communio/koinonia** in a straightforward way. The hurried reader can, if necessary, stop with this chapter. The following chapters go into more detail, grounding and expanding what is said in the first chapter.
>
> The **second chapter** describes the New Testament origins of the concept of communion and its appropriation by the ancient Church and the Lutheran Reformation. Here one can clearly see that **com-**

**munio** is not a new concept but is anchored deeply in the Christian and reformation tradition.

The **third chapter** explores the growing significance of this concept both for Lutheranism and for other churches. The questions before Lutherans today are being discussed in similar ways among other Christian World Communions and in the ecumenical movement. Here one can see both the common elements in the interpretation of **communio** by the different churches and the accents and aspects specific to each.

This study can be viewed as in part a summary and in part an elaboration of the larger study by Eugene L. Brand, **Toward a Lutheran Communion: Pulpit and Altar Fellowship** (LWF Report 26, 1988).

We thank those who provided critical remarks on earlier drafts of this study, particularly Prof. Georg Kretschmar (Munich) and Prof. Jürgen Roloff (Erlangen).

## CHAPTER I: THE MEANING OF "COMMUNIO/KOINONIA"

### 1. Why Are We Talking About "Communio/Koinonia"?

A sign of the times is the attempt to find community among Christians and churches and to overcome division, isolation, and complacency. Churches of the same confessional family come together across political and national boundaries, discovering anew that they belong together and have a responsibility for each other. Churches of different traditions and confessions seek unity beyond their historical divisions.

Although this movement toward greater unity has already borne much fruit, it has not yet reached its end. Churches of the same confessional family seek a fellowship that can deepen and strengthen their newly conscious unity. The reconciliation of previously divided churches cannot stop at partial agreements and peaceful coexistence; it pushes on to a fuller fellowship and communion.

Organizations and structures are only external forms of these efforts. At heart they concern the **quality and depth of our common life as Christians and as churches.**

• What is the basis of our fellowship and what holds it together?
• How do we experience this fellowship and how do we express it?
• How do we relate to each other, respecting our differences and sharing our needs and weaknesses, riches and joys?

- Can we depend on the stability and permanence of our fellowship?
- How do we maintain our fellowship: overcome conflicts, avoid discrimination, and resist isolation and splintering?
- Can we act together, not only for each other within the churches, but even more for others beyond the churches, for the world?

In relation to these questions about the **quality of our common life as Christians and as churches** the concept "**communio/koinonia**" has recently proved illuminating.

## 2. "Communio/Koinonia" Is Not a New Concept

The **New Testament** (see below, II.1) uses the term "**koinonia**" to speak of the communion of Christians with God the Father, of their communion with and in Christ, and of their fellowship in the Holy Spirit. This communion or fellowship is based on God's Word. It is a communion of worship and prayer. It means participation through Baptism in Christ's death and resurrection. The celebration of the Eucharist, where Christians gather to have communion with their Lord, is **koinonia. Koinonia** among Christians and congregations is expressed and realized in the sharing of joys and sorrows, needs and riches.

The concept "**communio/koinonia**" was also central for the **ancient Church** (see below, II.2). In the West the concept was taken up into the Apostles' Creed, which describes the Church as "the communion of saints." Like the New Testament, the ancient Church closely interrelated fellowship among churches and fellowship in the Eucharist as the meal of our common participation in the Lord and his salvation. Church fellowship must also be fellowship in the Eucharist, and both must be accompanied by fellowship in the apostolic faith.

The **Lutheran Reformation** (see below, II.3) appropriated the "**communio**" concept with which the Apostles' Creed describes the Church. The Church, "the communion of saints," is "the assembly of all believers." This "holy community" (**sancta communio**) is visible and recognizable especially in the proclamation of the Gospel in Word and sacraments. The "holy community" is gathered together and lives as the Holy Spirit awakens faith in Christ by communicating his saving work through Word and sacraments.

*"Communio/koinonia" is thus not a new or exclusively modern concept. As a biblical concept, it is part of the heritage of all churches and is familiar within all traditions. All churches should, indeed, must reflect on this concept as they seek to understand aright the quality of the common life of Christians and churches and to give this common life a concrete form.*

In fact, today **"communio"** plays a central role **in all churches and confessional families** when they state what they are as churches and what fellowship among Christians and churches means (see below, III.1).

**"Communio"** also plays a decisive role today **in the ecumenical movement and in ecumenical dialogues** as they seek to describe and realize the desired unity of the churches (see below, III.3).

### 3. What Does "Communio/Koinonia" Mean?

3.1. The Church is a human fellowship or communion (communio). Nevertheless, it is not a mere association on the basis of human conditions, interests, or efforts. Only as persons have communion with Christ through faith do they have communion with one another. Communion with Christ comes about through the preaching of the Gospel, which awakens and is embraced by faith, and through the sacraments, which strengthen and are received by faith.

*The concept "**communio**" means: The Church as a human fellowship or communion is always a communion in **Christ**. Its foundation is always communion with Christ through faith and participation in his saving work.*

3.2. Communion with Christ means participation in his passion and resurrection. Similarly, the communion of believers with each other implies that the joys and sufferings of individuals, their riches and poverty, their strengths and weaknesses, belong to all and are to be shared.

*The concept "**communio**" means: The fellowship or communion of believers is by nature a fellowship in **solidarity**. Solidarity is not optional. It impels a common participation in material and spiritual needs, in material and spiritual resources.*

3.3 Communion with Christ calls for a comprehensive commitment throughout one's life and work. Similarly, the communion of believers with each other implies commitment. It can grow by stages; but where it seeks full realization, it must be a mutually committed and thus reliable fellowship, always and everywhere, at both the local and universal levels. Its integrity permits no complacency, no self-segregation, no mutual condemnations, and no unjust discrimination.

The reliability, integrity, and mutual commitment within the fellowship impels concrete life and action:

in pulpit and altar fellowship. This fellowship presupposes fellowship in the confession of the faith and includes fellowship in the office of Word and sacraments.

in common actions and decisions which grow out of communion and agreement in faith and confession. In these actions and decisions, fellowship and agreement take on an authoritative character.

*The concept "**communio**" means: The fellowship or communion of believers is by nature a **committed** fellowship. Commitment is not optional; it impels the community toward common life and action.*

3.4. Communion with Christ is fellowship with the totality of believers throughout time and space. Similarly, the communion of believers with each other is a universal communion. No individual generation or epoch can separate itself from what has gone before. No separately organized church can isolate itself from the universal Church, which ties the churches together through its origin in the normative apostolic mission given by the risen Christ.

*The concept "**communio**" means: The fellowship or communion of believers is simultaneously particular and universal. Repeatedly, historical challenges arise in the face of which the relation to the universal Church is decisive for the particular church and its decisions. Conversely, the needs of a particular church demand action and decision from the universal fellowship.*

3.5. Communion with Christ includes in its totality and universality a multiplicity of individual pieties, gifts, and tasks. Similarly, the communion of believers with each other is a fellowship in which differences are not merely tolerated, but each is given room to realize its special excellence for the sake of the multiform mission of the Church.

*The concept "**communio**" means: The fellowship or communion of believers is not a coerced and prescribed uniformity. It realizes itself in a **variety of forms**. It lives and works through the multiplicity of gifts it receives and the variety of tasks placed before it.*

3.6. Christ seeks to bring all persons into communion with himself. Similarly, the fellowship or communion of believers opens itself to the world in missionary outreach, human service, and social action. Its being and action are a sign and instrument for the unity and peace of all humanity.

*The concept "**communio**" means: The fellowship or communion of believers looks beyond itself. It lives from its communion with the Lord, who is Lord and Savior of all creation and serves him as **sign and instrument for the salvation of the world**.*

## CHAPTER II: "COMMUNIO/KOINONIA" IN NEW TESTAMENT AND HISTORICAL PERSPECTIVE

### 1. "Koinonia" in the New Testament

"**Koinonia**" has a wide meaning in the New Testament. It ties together a number of basic concepts such as unity, life together, faith, and sharing.

It is also related to a variety of other New Testament images and concepts such as the "body of Christ" (e.g., 1 Cor. 12; Rom. 12), the Johannine expressions "being in" and "remaining in" (e.g., John 14:20, 23; 1 John 3:19-24; 4:15-16) and the parable of the vine and the branches (John 15:1-10) (1). The basic meaning of the verbal form, "**koinoneo**," is "to share, participate or have part in, have something in common or act together." The noun "**koinonia**" signifies "participation, fellowship, community." (2)

The different uses of "koinonia" and related words in the New Testament may be summarized briefly under the following headings:(3)

**1.1.** *Koinonia is participation in Christ.* According to a key text for understanding the concept, Christ is the basis and source of **koinonia** (1 Cor. 10:16-21). Through his broken body, he unites all those who share in him. Just as the broken body of Christ is one, it follows that all those who participate in sharing the bread and the cup become one. Through Christ, they are united and bound to him and to one another. The unity thus created by Christ is one that puts a demand on those incorporated into him. They are called to preserve and not to abuse the unity they have with him and with one another (v. 17). **Koinonia** is a gift. Its central point is participation in Christ. Those who take part in him become through him an indivisible unity–a communion.

From this concept "participation in Christ," Paul develops the image "the body of Christ." The two ideas are tied together (1 Cor. 10:17). The worshipping community, i.e., the Church, gathered around the Lord's Supper (1 Cor. 11:20-24) shares in Jesus Christ. (4) It is united with him into one body (1 Cor. 12:12f). Those who share in the Supper, and thus share in Jesus Christ, become one with him. The community is thus the body of Christ and participates in him and with one another. The many who are divided come together into one fellowship. Breaking bread together and sharing all things was thus a central factor in the life of the early Church (Acts 2:44-46; 4:35). This union with Christ is the basis for the commitment to solidarity with one another, mutual concern, and sharing.

**1.2.** *Koinonia is manifested above all in Baptism and in the celebration of the Lord's Supper.* Those who are baptized into Christ become one with him and with one another (Rom. 6:4-11; 1 Cor. 12:13). In the Lord's Supper, Christ is present as the host. The members share his body and his blood (1 Cor. 11:17-27) and thus become his companions. They are united with him. In this communion, there is no place for the party spirit which divides the community. Mutual consideration and care must be present in their gathering. They all become part of the communion that transcends all social or economic differences. In sharing the same bread and in drinking the same cup, they become one reconciled community. Their divisions are overcome and they become one body. This fellowship demands brotherly and sisterly conduct in the Church. Neglecting such conduct breaks up the **koinonia.** Being guests of the one Lord presupposes and leads to concern for and unity with one another.

Closely related is the "Fellowship in the Gospel" which signifies participation in and appropriation of the salvation made available by Christ (1 Cor. 9:23). It is receiving and sharing the faith in the company of God and others (Ph. 6). It expresses a state of close union with others in the proclamation of the Gospel and the attendant sufferings (2 Cor. 8:23; Phil. 1:5,7). Such fellowship means sharing the Word and the common prayer of the faithful (Acts 2:42). Such participants are **koinonoi** (partners) one of the other, and thus bound to one another (Phlm. 17; 2 Cor. 8:23). They extend each other "the right hand of fellowship" (Gal. 2:9) by which the unity of the Church is affirmed and solemnly sealed. The churches of the Jews and Gentiles, circumcised and uncircumcised, are brought into one fellowship through Christ.

1.3. *Koinonia signifies participation and sharing in the sufferings and joys of one another.* (5) Primarily, it means suffering with Christ and taking part in his cross (Phil. 3:10; Col. 1:24; 1 Peter 4:13; 5:1). The spiritual union that binds Christ and the believer means that the believers identify and suffer with Christ (Rom. 8:17; Gal. 2:19). **Koinonia** is sharing in the sufferings of Christ and in the sufferings of the fellow believer (Heb. 10:33). Mutuality of suffering is grounded in participation in Christ. A church becomes one with the apostle in this suffering (2 Cor. 1: 6,7; 7:3); the Philippian church shares in the sufferings of the apostle Paul (Phil. 4:14). This connection is expressed concretely when a church provides for the material needs of the apostle and supports him through its gifts (vv. 15,16).

1.4. *Koinonia is expressed in sharing what one has with others.* (6) This aspect of the meaning of "**koinonia**" is seen in Paul's collections among the churches in Asia for the church in Jerusalem (Rom. 15:26; 2 Cor. 9:13). This collection was a visible sign and symbol of unity of the different churches, in this case Jews and Gentiles. It was an expression of the essence of the Gospel of Jesus Christ. "**Koinonia**" here carries the dynamic sense of making the other a participant in one's riches through a contribution to the other's well-being. The monetary collection is itself called "fellowship" (**koinonia**, Rom. 15:26; cp. Heb. 13:16). The material gifts are related to the spiritual gifts in such a way that they flow between one another (Rom. 15:27). There is reciprocal sharing to meet the needs of each community and sustain the whole. There is a mutual giving and receiving on the basis of a fellowship that already exists. (7) Christians are exhorted to share (Gal. 6:6; Rom. 12:13).

This sharing does not require riches but occurs even amid "extreme poverty" as among the churches in Macedonia (2 Cor. 8:1-4), who first gave themselves to the Lord and to us by the will of God." This accords with spirit of Christ, who himself "became poor for your sake, to make you rich out of his poverty" (2 Cor. 8:9). The giving based on **koinonia** is an act of faith in God and not merely an act of generosity. It results from a relation which constrains the parties to empathize and share the resources with one another (Rom. 12:13; Heb. 13:16) because of their unity in the Lord.

1.5. *Christ creates **koinonia** because he is in fellowship with the Father.* Father and Son are one (e.g., John 10:3; 14:9-11). This unity enables the believers to have fellowship with God and fellowship with one another (1 John 1:3,6,7; cp. 2 Peter 1:4). It is God who calls "the saints" into "the fellowship of his Son" (1 Cor. 1:9). This is also a fellowship in and through the Holy Spirit (2 Cor. 13:13; Phil 2:1).

1.6. *****Koinonia** has an eschatological dimension.* Not only is it a present reality, but it points to a greater and more complete fulfillment at the endtime (1 Cor. 9:23). Even if the present is lived in suffering, there is still hope of sharing in a glory that will come (Rom. 8:17; 1 Peter 4:13; 5:1). There is a firm faith that sharing in suffering will be followed by sharing in consolation (2 Cor. 1:7).

## 2. "Koinonia/Communio" in the Ancient Church

As in the New Testament, so in the ancient Church the communion of the believers with the triune God and with each other was described in a variety of ways. In earliest times, "**koinonia**," "**communio**," and derived words referred particularly to common participation in Christ in the Eucharist. "**Koinonia**" and "**communio**" could thus become titles for the Eucharist.

An important example is the formula "**communion of the saints**" (**communio sanctorum**), known in the West particularly through its inclusion in the Apostles' Creed. This phrase can already be found in texts from the late 4th century. The earliest examples are from the Eastern church. (8) Most likely, the phrase originally referred to the communion in sacred things, i.e., participation in Christ through the consecrated bread and wine. This interpretation, with its allusion to Paul's comments about **koinonia** with Christ's body and blood (1 Cor. 10:16), can also be found in the Western church. In the West, however, the phrase came gradually to mean what it does today: the communion of Christians one with another, not only within the earthly Church, but with the faithful throughout the ages.

The two interpretations of "**communio sanctorum**" are closely interrelated—participation in the eucharistic gifts and the communion or fellowship of the faithful. The communion of the faithful is rooted in their connection with the crucified and resurrected Christ and is realized in their common unity with Christ in the celebration of the Eucharist. Those who partake of the one bread become one body (cp. 1 Cor. 10:17) and enter into communion one with another. *Fellowship in the Eucharist* is unthinkable, however, without *fellowship in the faith*. Only the baptized who share the same faith can come to the table of the Lord. According to Justin Martyr (ca. 155), one can partake of the Eucharist only if one "believes that the things we teach are true, and has received the washing for the the forgiveness of sins and for rebirth, and lives as Christ handed down to us" (First Apology, 66.1). This faith takes on a normative form through councils and synods. The faithful are bound together in their agreement with this teaching, which expresses their membership in the Church. Those who do not accept the faith in this normative, doctrinal form exclude themselves from the **communio**. They are practically, if not always formally, excommunicated and separated from the universal fellowship of the Church.

The same is true at the level of relations between churches. A church which does not find in another church that which it holds as fundamental cannot have fellowship in the Eucharist with that church. If the unity of the body of Christ has been broken, then common participation in the eucharistic celebration of Christ's body and blood is impossible. In the ancient Church, the Lord's Supper was never seen as a means to the re-establishment of a lost unity; it is always the sign of a present unity.

Closely connected was the understanding of the *bishop* as a sign of the **communio** prior to all divisions, first locally, then regionally, and finally universally. Ignatius of Antioch (ca. 110) wrote that a valid Eucharist can only be celebrated by a bishop or his representative (Smyr. 8.1). They are blessed, he said, who are as closely bound to their bishop "as the Church is to Jesus Christ, and as Jesus Christ is with the Father, so that unity and harmony can prevail everywhere" (Eph. 5.1). It was repeatedly emphasized that fellowship in the Church is realized through subordination to the legitimate bishop: "The bishop is in the Church and the Church in the bishop; if one is not with the bishop, then one is not in the Church" (Cyprian, Ep. 66.8). As a consequence, the bishops as a whole were increasingly viewed as the visible expression of the unity of the Church. The local church then is in communion with other churches through its bishop (**communio ecclesiastica**). As Irenaeus of Lyon (ca. 190) emphasized, the bishops as successors of the apostles are bearers of the true apostolic tradition (Adv. Haer. III.3.1-2). Doctrinally suspect bishops became all the more vehemently opposed, for their appearance directly threatened the unity of the entire Church as founded by Christ.

### 3. "Communio/Fellowship" in the Lutheran Reformation

The application of the "**communio**" concept to the Church was self-evident for the Reformation in light of the witness of the New Testament and the ancient Church. CA 7 describes the "one holy Christian Church" as the "*assembly of all believers*." This "assembly" is *identical with the "communion of saints"* of which the Apostles' Creed speaks (Apol. 7.8). The Large Catechism also identifies the "communion of saints" with this "little holy flock or community" (LC II.51). (9)

The specific emphasis of the Reformation – that the Church is an assembly, people, or community of believers, and not primarily a hierarchical institution (Apol. 7.23) – does not reduce the Church to a mere gathering of individuals. CA 7 thus adds to its description: The Church is "the assembly of all believers *among whom the Gospel is preached in its purity and the holy sacraments are administered according to the Gospel.*" An assembly or community is Church because of an event that occurs within it, the proclamation of the Gospel in Word and sacraments. Through this proclamation of the Gospel Christ is present in his saving power and is grasped by faith. As faith unites believers with Christ, they are justified before God, freed from the power of sin, and made members of Christ's body, the Church.

In this reformation interpretation, the meaning of "**koinonia/communio**" for the New Testament and the ancient Church comes to full expression: *The Church as a human community is based solely on communion in faith with Christ.* Luther said that "to have communion or fellowship" means not simply "having some relationship with another person." Rather it signifies that "many persons share or eat or partake of one common thing."(10)

As the assembly of all who participate in Christ through faith, the Church is a "fellowship [which] is *inward, spiritual, and invisible, for it is in the heart.*"(11) The Church is "mainly an association of faith and of the Holy Spirit in men's hearts" (Apol. 7.5) which extends through space and time. As such a "spiritual communion," the Church is not however simply invisible. The Church is not "some Platonic republic" (Apol 7.20) which is nowhere to be found. As a "spiritual communion," the Church is simultaneously a "*fellowship [which] is outward, physical, and visible.*"(12) The Church can be seen and experienced particularly in the community's concrete preaching of the Gospel and its celebration of the sacraments. In these easily perceivable events, the Church comes to be; without them the Church cannot exist. The communion which is the Church is thus a *visible communion in the proclamation of the Word and the celebration of the sacraments.* At the inter-congregational or inter-church level, this communion finds expression in what would later be called "*altar and pulpit fellowship.*"

Such "altar and pulpit fellowship" includes *communion or fellowship in the divinely instituted office of ministry* (CA 5). This office is commissioned to proclaim the Gospel in Word and sacraments and at the same time to *help protect and maintain communion.* Thus the office, exercised by pastors or bishops, is, by divine right, to exclude from and admit to the visible communion (CA 28.21; Treatise 60-62).

Since justifying faith is awakened and the Church is gathered only by the *pure* preaching of the Gospel and the *evangelical* celebration of the sacraments, communion and its preservation require agreement in the right understanding of the Gospel (CA 7). The Reformation sought such agreement primarily by means of explicit *confessional consensus* documents adopted by congregations and churches. In such a *confessional communion* the communion of churches also finds visible expression.

While the communion of Christians with one another is grounded in common participation in Christ, it is also a community of mutual commitment and participation. Luther says: "This fellowship is twofold: on the one hand we partake of Christ and all saints; on the other hand we permit all Christians to be partakers of us, in whatever way they and we are able."(13) Thus *ethical and social action for the good of the neighbor* is also an expression and realization of communion.

## CHAPTER III: "COMMUNIO" IN THE CONTEMPORARY ECUMENICAL CONTEXT

### 1.1 "Communio" in Catholicism

The concept "**communio**" plays an important role in the description of the Church in contemporary Roman Catholic theology. It appeals to New Testament and ancient Church understandings and serves as a corrective to more juridical or legal understandings of the Church. The "**communio**" concept has been called "*the central and fundamental idea*" of the ecclesiology developed by Vatican II.(14)

As in New Testament and ancient theology, Catholic theology interrelates the believers' participation in grace and the divine life and their participation in the communion of the Church. Personal communion with God always creates a "communion of the faithful" one with another.(15)

This communion is realized through the preaching of the Gospel (16) and the administration of the sacraments, (17) especially the Eucharist. "Partaking of the body of the Lord in the breaking of the Eucharistic bread, we are taken up into communion with Him and with one another." (18)

The Church as **communio** is thus essentially a "eucharistic communion," (19) which itself presupposes a fellowship in faith. This communion is "perfected . . . in the confession of one faith, in the common celebration of divine worship, and in the fraternal harmony of the family of God."(20)

At the local level, this "communion of the faithful" is made concrete in the particular local church (e.g., diocese) grounded in the Eucharist and led by the bishop. At the universal level, communion is made concrete as the *communion of local churches*, in which there is room for legitimate diversity.(21)

At every level, a *personal office of leadership* is essential to communion. At the local level, there is the bishop, standing in historical succession and in collegial relations with other bishops.(22) At the universal level, this office is the papacy, with its primacy of teaching and jurisdiction,(23) under whom the bishops can gather together in a council.(24)

Compared to the Lutheran understanding, the specificity of the Roman Catholic understanding of "**communio**" lies in the central role played by the Eucharist. Even more, the "communion of the faithful" has a determinate form, among whose absolutely essential elements are certain offices of leadership, that of the bishop and of the pope.

### 1.2. "Communio" in Orthodoxy

The Orthodox Church is a *communion of churches*, bound together neither by a centralized organization nor through a single official. (25) As primates, patriarchs and archbishops do function as signs of the unity of their churches. The ecumenical patriarch of Constantinople does have a priority of honor as "first among equals." Nevertheless, the Orthodox churches are unified in love and peace only through communion in faith and sacraments.

The faith which is the basis of this communion is the faith deepened by the interpretations of the Fathers of the ancient Church and affirmed by the *seven ecumenical councils*. For the Orthodox, a council is "not an authority equipped with power to rule over the church"(26) but rather a witness to the Church's self-consciousness. As is shown by several examples in church history, a council takes on its ecumenical, and thus normative, character only after its decisions have been received as true by the whole of the people of the Church. From this perspective clergy and laity are on the same level; and no authoritative, not to mention infallible, teaching office can take the place of this spiritual unanimity.

The inner catholicity of the Church is the concern here, sometimes referred to by the Russian word "**sobornost**." Led by the Holy Spirit and gathered around Christ their head, the many faithful have a free common existence, each having a particular gift of grace. As unity and multiplicity are joined together, the life of the Church mirrors the life of the triune God.

The *office of bishop* plays a central role in this process by which the independence of each Orthodox church does not disturb the doctrinal and eucharistic unity of the whole. Standing in apostolic succession, the bishops express the unity of the Church through their ties to one another. This unity in the bishops comes to expression particularly in a *council*, for which the Orthodox are at present preparing. Nevertheless, councils are only one aspect of communion in faith and sacraments. Communion is both an important and a comprehensive concept for the Orthodox. It concerns all members of the Church and can be experienced only by participation in the life of the Church through the power of the Holy Spirit.

This understanding differentiates itself in a variety of ways from Lutheran understandings of communion: for example, in the absolutely central position of the eucharistic celebration, in the significance given to the seven ancient councils, and not least in the office of the bishop in historical succession, which is unconditionally necessary for communion or fellowship between churches. A certain similarity to Lutheran understandings exists, however, insofar as communio is understood as a *spiritual* phenomenon and therefore by nature contains a dimension of openness and freedom.

### 1.3. "Communio" in Anglicanism

The Anglican churches refer to themselves as a *communion* perhaps more than any other group of churches. Historically, the churches of the Anglican Communion all derive in some way from the Church of England and thus share elements of a common cultural heritage. Theologically, they all affirm the four elements of the Lambeth Quadrilateral: Scripture as the ultimate rule of faith, the Apostles' and Nicene Creeds, the sacraments of Baptism and the Lord's Supper, and the historic episcopate. The common affirmation of these four elements is held to be necessary for the visible unity of the Church and thus necessary for communion between churches.

*Communion in the episcopate* has been particularly important for Anglicans. The communion of the bishops throughout the world and in history realized in episcopal succession focuses and serves the unity of the Church. Thus, of the four "embodiments and agents of unity" within the Anglican Communion, three focus on the episcopate: the "primacy of honor" of the Archbishop of Canterbury, the meeting of the Primates of the Anglican churches, and the Lambeth Conferences of Anglican bishops from around the world. (The fourth, the Anglican Consultative Council, includes also laity and clergy other than bishops.) (27) The emphasis on the episcopate as servant and sign of unity should not obscure, however, the deep Anglican conviction that communion is first and foremost in Christ, his Gospel and sacraments.(28)

Like the Lutheran communion, the Anglican communion is made up of autonomous churches (or provinces). None of the "agents of unity" can make decisions for a particular Anglican church or province. Today Anglicans are struggling with questions of what communion requires. When should a church decide a question for itself without consultation with other churches? When should it consult other churches before acting? Are there any questions that should be settled only by some consensus of the churches? If there are any such questions, what international, communion-wide structures are appropriate for dealing with them? These questions of authority are at the center of recent Anglican discussions of the nature of the Church as communion. (29)

While sharing much with Lutherans in their understanding of communion, Anglicans are distinguished from them by an emphasis on communion in the office of the historic episcopate.

### 1.4. "Communio" in the Reformed Churches

The center of the Reformed understanding of "**communio**" is the *communion of the faithful with Christ*. Through Word and the Holy Spirit, the faithful enter communion with Christ and become members of his body.(30) To share in Christ is simultaneously to share in the living communion of the Church. (31)

More than the Lutheran tradition, the Reformed tradition has emphasized the distinction between the *invisible Church*, the "communion of saints," and the visible Church, the community existing here and now. The invisible Church is the perfect communion of the elect, the angels and the blessed. The visible Church, however, is a community of both the faithful and the hypocritical. (32) Calvin, the Reformed confessions, and recent Reformed theology emphasize that the two must be distinguished but not separated. (33) Their unity is given in Christ, the head of the Body. Preaching and the sacraments ground and nourish individual faith and thus also the communion of the faithful in Christ and their unity. (34) Calvin refers to the Church as mother of the faithful. The Church itself contributes to the communion of the individual with Christ, not least through the special ministry instituted within it. (35) This emphasis has receded among contemporary Reformed churches in favor of an emphasis on Christ as bond of communion.

The Reformed tradition has also characteristically emphasized that communion means *common care and concern*. Calvin says that to call the Church a "communion of saints" is "as if one said that the saints were gathered into the society of Christ on the principle that whatever benefits God confers upon them, they should in turn share with one another." (36) Closely related is the insistence that communion with Christ implies a *responsibility for a new community among all humanity*. The Reformed tradition has constantly emphasized that the Church is by nature a community of witness and service. Here perhaps the Reformed tradition is different from the Lutheran tradition, though only in its emphasis.

The Reformed and Lutheran streams of the Reformation have fundamentally agreed in their understanding of communion. Their differing emphases have never been church-dividing.

## 2. "Communio" in Lutheranism (37)

Since the second half of the nineteenth century, Lutherans have become increasingly conscious, first, of the worldwide Lutheran communion and then of the broader ecumenical communion. Particularly since the founding of the LWF, the concept of "*communion*" or "*church fellowship*" has played an increasingly important, even programmatic role. In the process, New Testament and ancient Church understandings of "**koinonia**" and "**communio**" have been newly appropriated. (38)

Three convictions going back to the Reformers (see II.3) have remained relatively constant in this quest for communion:

*First, communion between churches must be communion in the confession of the faith* [**Kirchengemeinschaft ist Bekenntnisgemeinschaft**]. Interchurch aid in time of need and common missionary work and social service are important; they mediate the experience and consciousness of the reality of communion. Nevertheless, communion is founded in our common faith in the one proclaimed Gospel. This common faith should find expression in a confession which orients the preaching and sacramental practice of the Church in accord with the Gospel. Common confessions have been the decisive mark of Lutheran unity. Individual Lutheran churches, as well as regional and worldwide Lutheran fellowships, have stated a doctrinal basis which includes, after the Bible and the Creeds, the fundamental Lutheran confessions. As Lutherans have sought communion with other traditions, a consensus in the commonly confessed faith has been essential to their quest.

*Second, communion in preaching and sacraments is essential to communion between churches.* Communion is realized in the living proclamation of the Gospel in Word and sacraments. Thus, Lutheran communion has focused on "pulpit and altar fellowship" and the mutual recognition of churchly office which that implies, even though communion also seeks realization in other aspects of church life. In general, Lutheran churches have been and are in pulpit and altar fellowship because of their common confession. On occasion fellowship has been lacking because of theological divergences or non-theological factors. Such cases have been seen as abnormal or unacceptable.

*Third, communion between churches does not require uniformity in merely human church structures, forms of worship, or church practices, but calls for freedom and legitimate diversity in these areas.* Within the Lutheran communion can be found different church structures (both episcopal and non-episcopal), different liturgical traditions, different theological streams, and different forms of piety.

Alongside these shared and constant convictions, however, have been debated questions:

*Does "communion in the confession of the faith" require the common acceptance of the same confessional text?* Not only recent theological reflection, but also decisions by the LWF and its member churches have answered this question "No."(39) The need for a communion in the confession of the faith can be met through a consensus in the understanding of the Gospel and its proclamation in Word and Sacrament. This consensus, however, should be explicitly formulated or at least be capable of formulation.

*Does the common confession of the LWF member churches permit, or even demand, a common declaration of altar and pulpit fellowship?* This question was answered "Yes" by the LWF Assembly in Budapest (1984) in its "Statement on the Self-Understanding and Task of the Lutheran World Federation." This decision was expressed in the concept of "Lutheran communion" and embodied in a constitutional amendment (Art. III,1).

*In what forms of common life is communion expressed and realized?* In its Budapest "Statement on Self-Understanding," the LWF stated that communion "finds its visible expression" not only in altar and pulpit fellowship, but also "in common witness and service, in the joint fulfillment of the missionary task, and in openness to ecumenical cooperation, dialog, and community." Such a communion must be "a mutually committed fellowship."

*What kinds of common actions and decisions must the Lutheran communion of churches be able to take, particularly through the LWF as its instrument and expression?* The LWF has defined itself as a "free association of Lutheran churches" (Constitution, Art. III,1). But can a communion of churches, joined by a common confession in pulpit and altar fellowship, find adequate organizational expression only in a "free association?" Can a "free association" of churches do what the LWF has in fact done, declaring that apartheid creates in Southern Africa a special situation of confession and suspending the membership of two Southern Africa churches?(40) Common action has been taken, and thus necessarily common decisions made, since the founding of the LWF. Otherwise the LWF would have been incapable of the common witness and service for which its Constitution calls (Art. III). The problem arises when a decision or action claims to commit authoritatively the entire communion and its member churches. Is such a decision authoritative only if and when it is received and agreed to by the individual churches? Or do such decisions *as decisions of the communion* already commit the individual churches? About what matters and under what conditions can such decisions be made? Who would make such decisions and by what process? These and similar questions are still being debated. The concept of communion itself implies no particular answer to these questions, but life in communion does require some forms of common and authoritative decision making. (41)

"Communion" [**Kirchengemeinschaft**] has been important not only for Lutheran unity but also for Lutheran participation in *ecumenical discussions and efforts.* This became particularly evident in 1977 at the LWF Assembly in Dar es Salaam, when "unity in reconciled diversity" was adopted as a guiding principle in Lutheran ecumenical efforts. (42) This concept was developed further, with explicit use of the concept of communion, in the 1984 Budapest Assembly statement on "The Unity We Seek." (43) Especially in the 1980's, bilateral dialogues involving Lutherans have turned to concepts of communion to explicate their understanding of the ecumenical goal. (44)

### 3. "Communio" in Ecumenical Dialogues

1. The concept "communion" has been of decisive significance for the modern ecumenical movement. For all Christian traditions, the Church is simultaneously a communion with Christ in the Holy Spirit, a communion of churches or congregations, and a communion of the faithful. "Communion" thus describes not only the essence of the individual churches but also the unity sought. The concept entered ecumenical dialogues particularly when attempts were made to gather together the initial results and take concrete steps toward a growing together of the churches. It became clear that "unity" needed both interpretation and qualification. In the attempt to understand more precisely and to live out more faithfully the unity of the Church, the understanding of the Church as **communio** readily suggested itself, even if this understanding varied according to tradition and situation (see above III.1).

2. The *World Council of Churches* led the way in the ecumenical development of the concept of communion. The Assembly in New Delhi (1961) described the unity we seek in terms of communion:

> We believe that the unity which is both God's will and his gift to his Church is being made visible as all in each place who are baptized into Jesus Christ and confess him as Lord and Savior are brought by the Holy Spirit into one fully committed fellowship, holding the one apostolic faith, preaching the one Gospel, breaking the one bread, joining in common prayer, and having a corporate life reaching out in witness and service to all.

In the Assembly's "Commentary," this description is expanded:

> The word 'fellowship' (**koinonia**) [i.e., communion] has been chosen because it describes what the Church truly is. 'Fellowship' clearly implies that the Church is not merely an institution or organization. It is a fellowship of those who are called together by the Holy Spirit and in Baptism confess Christ as Lord and Savior. They are thus 'fully committed' to him and to one another. Such a fellowship means for those who participate in it nothing less than a renewed mind and spirit, a full participation in common praise and prayer, the shared realities of penitence and forgiveness, mutuality in suffering and joy, listening together to the same Gospel, responding in faith, obedience, and service, joining in the one mission of Christ in the world, a self-forgetting love for all for whom Christ died, and the reconciling grace which breaks down every wall of race, color, caste, tribe, sex, class, and nation. Neither does this 'fellowship' imply a rigid uniformity of structure, organization, or government. A lively variety marks corporate life in the one Body of one Spirit.(45)

A few years later, the Decree on Ecumenism of *Vatican II* said similarly: "It is the Holy Spirit . . . who brings about that marvelous communion of the faithful and joins them together so intimately in Christ that He is the principle of the Church's unity. . . . Christ perfects the people's communion in unity."(46)

3. In more recent years, "**communio**," "communion," and "church fellowship" have become increasingly important in the *ecumenical dialogues*. Nevertheless, different understandings of "**communio**" appear when one tries more precisely to describe which elements are constitutive for communion or fellowship among churches and how these elements are to be related to each other (see above, III.1 and 2).

3.1. The most extensive understanding of "**communio**" is found in the *Orthodox-Roman Catholic dialogue*. Here emphasis falls both on communion in faith, which is necessary for unity, and communion in the sacraments, which is a condition and fruit of communion in faith. These two forms of communion are two sides of a single reality. (47) Each side receives a characteristic interpretation in the dialogue. On the one hand, faith includes "the totality of doctrine and church practice." (48) Among the criteria for this faith is "the continuity of the tradition" (along with the doxological and soteriological meanings of the faith). (49) On the other hand, agreement in faith makes possible communion in the sacraments, which finds its highest expression in the Eucharist. Each Eucharist in each place is the full expression of the full, true communion of all local churches in the one Christ, which is the mystery of the Church.(50)

3.2. The conditions for true communion are formulated in a more differentiated way in the *dialogues among Rome and the churches of the Reformation*. Full communion includes communion in Word, in the sacraments, and in ministry. Different dialogues, however, spell out this assertion in different ways.

The *Anglican-Roman Catholic dialogue* has explicitly focused on "**koinonia**" as the central concept for understanding the Church and its unity. **Koinonia** is both participation in the saving work of Christ and also the communion of Christians with each other. **Koinonia** is "grounded in the Word of God preached, believed, and obeyed;" "established" through Baptism; and "sustained" through the Eucharist. "Full visible communion" between churches requires "mutual recognition of sacraments and ministry, together with the common acceptance of a universal primacy." (51)

The *Lutheran-Roman Catholic dialogue* has emphasized the same constitutive elements of communion but does not speak of the necessity of a universal office of unity.(52) Communion is a gift of God's grace, mediated through Word, the sacraments, and the indispensable office of ministry. It expresses itself in the unity of faith, hope, and love and seeks a visible form. This form does not require uniformity but rather allows for legitimate diversity. In accord with the image and analogy of the triune God, this unity encompasses all Christians and is oriented toward the unity of all humanity. (53)

The realization of such communion is a step-by-step process of coming together. Decisive steps have already been taken. The most difficult problem remains the still incomplete communion in ministerial office. Here special weight is placed on the contention that only within communion in ministry can communion in Word and sacraments take on its full, visible form and normative character. (54)

The still imperfect communion and ministry is a central problem also in the dialogues between Rome and other Reformation churches. (55)

3.3. In *dialogues among the Reformation churches*, the communion sought between the churches has predominantly been understood as communion in Word and sacraments and described by the phrases "church fellowship" (**Kirchengemeinschaft**) or "full communion."

A significant example is the *communion or fellowship between Lutheran and Reformed*. This communion is already a reality in Europe through the Leuenberg Agreement (1973). (56) Its extension throughout the world has been recommended by the international dialogue. (57) A full agreement in Word and sacraments is the necessary and sufficient condition of communion (see CA 7). (58) This agreement is established through a doctrinal consensus about Word and sacraments, which includes the lifting of earlier doctrinal condemnations. Communion in Word and sacraments (i.e., pulpit and altar fellowship) includes a mutual recognition of ordination. Here again a communion in ministry is important, even if clearly subordinate to communion in Word and sacraments. The communion declared, however, must then be realized in the concrete life of the churches. It impels the churches toward communion in witness and service in the world.

A different weight is given to communion in ministry in the *Lutheran-Anglican dialogue*. Among Reformation churches, the Anglicans place particular emphasis on episcopacy in historic succession as a bond of communion (see above, III.1.3.), without denying the apostolicity of churches not in such a succession. Full communion is more than communion in Word and sacraments; it includes communion in ministry. (59) Lutheran-Anglican dialogues have agreed, however, that office and succession do not stand on the same level as the other elements of communion, Word and sacraments. This communion finds expression also in a communion in mission and service to the world.(60)

This necessary communion in witness has been consistently emphasized by the dialogues among the Reformation churches.

NOTES

1. C. H. Dodd, **The Johannine Epistles**, The Moffatt New Testament Commentary (London: Hodder and Stoughton, 1975), pp. 6-9. To these may be added the Old Testament concept of "corporate personality," i.e., "basic human solidarity among all the sons of Adam," and the New Testament expressions that contain the term "with" (Greek: **syn**) as found e.g. in Rom. 6:3-11; 8:17; 2 Cor. 7:3; Col. 3:1; Eph. 2:6. See Michael McDermott, "The Biblical Doctrine of **Koinonia**," **Biblische Zeitschrift**, 19 N.F. (1975):66.

2. McDermott, p. 65.

3. Cf. F. Hauck, art. "**koinonia**" in **Theological Dictionary of the New Testament**, ed. by Gerhard Kittel (Grand Rapids: Eerdmans, 1965), vol. 3, pp. 1746ff. Josef Hainz, **Koinonia: "Kirche" als Gemeinschaft bei Paulus. Biblische Untersuchungen** (Regensburg: Verlag Friedrich Pustet, 1982).

4. Paul S. Minear, **Images of the Church in the New Testament** (London: Lutterworth Press, 1961), p. 185.

5. Schuyler Brown, "**Koinonia** as the Basis of New Testament Ecclesiology?" **One in Christ**, 12 (1976): p. 163.

6. Georg Kretschmar, "Gemeinschaft der Heiligen im Neuen Testament und in der frühen Kirche." **Una Sancta**, 43 (1988): 266-276.

7. Eugene L. Brand, **Toward a Lutheran Communion**, p. 14.

8. Werner Elert, **Eucharist and Church Fellowship in the First Four Centuries** (St. Louis: Concordia, 1966), pp. 8, 209-218.

9. As is shown in this and other texts, the concepts "communio" and "congregatio" are equivalent and synonymous: "**sanctorum congregatiuncula et communio.**"

10. "Confession Concerning Christ's Supper," **LW-AE,** vol. 37, p. 356 (WA 26,493).

11. "A Sermon on the Ban," **LW-AE,** vol. 39, p. 7 (WA 6,64;1,639).

12. "A Sermon on the Ban," p. 8.

13. "The Blessed Sacrament of the Holy and True Body of Christ and the Brotherhoods," **LW-AE,** vol. 35, p. 67 (WA 2,754).

14. 1985 Extraordinary Synod of Bishops.

15. Vatican II, Decree on Ecumenism, 2.

16. Vatican II, Decree on Ecumenism, 2; Constitution on the Sacred Liturgy, 51; Dogmatic Constitution on Divine Revelation, 21.

17. Vatican 2, Dogmatic Constitution on the Church, 7; cp. Decree on Ecumenism, 22.

18. Vatican II, Dogmatic Constitution on the Church, 7.

19. Vatican II, Decree on Ecumenism, 22.

20. Vatican II, Decree on Ecumenism, 2.

21. Vatican II, Dogmatic Constitution on the Church, 13, 23, 26, and passim; cp. Code of Canon Law, cc. 368f.

22. Code of Canon Law, c. 369.

23. Cp. Vatican II, Dogmatic Constitution on the Church, 22; Decree on the Bishops' Pastoral Office in the Church, 4.

24. Cp. Vatican II, Dogmatic Constitution on the Church, 22.

25. Among the Orthodox churches, one distinguishes between autocephalous and autonomous churches on that basis of their different organizational status. These often national churches are often called "local churches," although they are not "local churches" in the usual sense of a diocese. See John Zizioulas, **Being as Communion** (London: 1985), pp. 251-253.

26. Alexander Schmemann, "Der Begriff des Primates in der orthodoxen Ekklesiologie," in **Der Primat des Petrus in der orthodoxen Kirche**, ed. Boris Bobrinskoy (Zürich: 1961), p. 136.

27. On these bonds of unity, see **The Truth Shall Make You Free: The Lambeth Conference 1988**: The Reports, Resolutions & Pastoral Letters from the Bishops (London: Anglican Consultative Council, 1988), pp. 110f.

28. See, e.g., Archbishop Runcie's Opening Address to the 1988 Lambeth Conference, in **The Lambeth Conference 1988**, especially p. 19.

29. See here especially the so-called Eames Report, **Report of the Archbishop of Canterbury's Commission on Communion and Women in the Episcopate** (London: Anglican Consultative Council, 1989).

30. Heidelberg Catechism, Q. 32. See also question 31.

31. Heidelberg Catechism, Qq. 54f. Westminster Confession, XXVI,1.2.

32. John Calvin, **Institutes of the Christian Religion**, IV.1.2-7; Westminster Confession, XXV,1-2,4-5.

33. John Calvin, **Institutes of the Christian Religion**, IV.1.3. See also the Geneva Catechism, Part I, 92-105, as well as the Heidelberg Catechism, Qq. 54f. Among recent Reformed theologians, see K. Barth, **Church Dogmatics**, IV/1, p. 669.

34. Calvin, **Institutes**, IV.1.1; 2.4; and Heidelberg Catechism, Qq. 75, 77.

35. **Institutes**, IV.1.4; IV.3.

36. **Institutes**, IV.1.3. See also Heidelberg Catechism, Q. 55.

37. See here especially Eugene L. Brand, **Toward a Lutheran Communion**.

38. In the work of the LWF Theological Commission in years before the Assemblies in Minneapolis (1957) and Helsinki (1963), the concept of "communion" or "fellowship" moved steadily to the center. See **The Unity of the Church: A Symposium**, Papers presented to the Commissions on Theology and Liturgy of the Lutheran World Federation (Rock Island, Illinois: Augustana Press, 1957) and **The Nature of the Lutheran World Federation**: Preparatory Document no. 4, 4th LWF Assembly (Geneva: LWF, 1963). Much of this discussion took place in German and thus spoke of "Kirchengemeinschaft." "Gemeinschaft" can be translated into English as "fellowship," "community," or "communion." Since the term "*Kirchengemeinschaft*" took up important aspects of the New Testament and ancient Church idea of "*communio*" and "*koinonia*," here it will be translated as "communion." This connection with earlier concepts can be seen in **Koinonia: Arbeiten des Oekumenischen Ausschusses der Vereinigten Evangelisch-Lutherischen Kirche Deutschlands zur Frage der Kirchen-und Abendmahlsgemeinschaft** (Berlin: Lutherisches Verlagshaus, 1957).

39. Note, e.g., the admission of Indonesian churches into the LWF, although they do not recognize the Augsburg Confession; the Evian "Statement Concerning the Attitude of the LWF to Churches in Union Negotiations" (**Sent into the World**: Proceedings of the Fifth Assembly of the Lutheran World Federation, pp. 142f); and the acceptance of the Leuenberg Agreement by the majority of European Lutheran churches, bringing them into communion with churches with Reformed and United confessional bases.

40. For a discussion of this action, see **The Debate on Status Confessionis: Studies in Christian Political Theology**, LWF Studies (Geneva, 1983).

41. The Budapest Assembly stated that "the unity we seek . . . is a committed fellowship, able to make common decisions and to act in common." ("Statement on the Unity We Seek," **Budapest 1984**, p. 175.)

42. This action was the fruition of discussions going back to the work of the LWF Theology Commission before the Minneapolis LWF Assembly (1957) and even more before the Helsinki Assembly (1963). See the references above in nt. 38, especially "The Nature of the Lutheran World Federation."

43. See **Budapest 1984**: Official Proceedings of the Seventh Assembly of the Lutheran World Federation, **LWF Report** 19/20 (1985): 175.

44. See especially the Lutheran-Roman Catholic documents **Ways to Community** (1981) and **Facing Unity** (1985), the Lutheran-Reformed document **Toward Church Fellowship** (1989), and the Lutheran-Anglican **Niagara Report** (1987).

45. Report of the Section on Unity, Third Assembly of the World Council of Churches, §§2, 11.

46. Vatican II, Decree on Ecumenism, 2-4; here §2.

47. See especially the second document of the international Orthodox-Roman Catholic dialogue, **Faith, Sacraments, and the Unity of the Church**, Bari, 1987, §36.

48. Faith, Sacraments, and the Unity of the Church, 6,7.

49. Faith, Sacraments, and the Unity of the Church, 28-32.

50. Faith, Sacraments, and the Unity of the Church, 23f and 34ff.

51. Preface to the Final Report of ARCIC I (1981). The preface contains an extended analysis of the concept of **koinonia**.

52. See especially the documents which address this theme: **Ways to Community** (1980) and **Facing Unity** (1985).

53. See here **Ways to Community**, §§1-52.

54. The question of communion in ministry is one of the foci of the document **Facing Unity**. See especially §§ 86ff.

55. E.g., the Methodist-Roman Catholic dialogues, 4th series, 1982-86, sections 29-76 and the Reformed-Roman Catholic dialogue **The Presence of Christ in Church and World** (1977), sections 93-108.

56. On the understanding of communion or fellowship, especially in the Leuenberg Agreement, see H. Meyer, "Zur Entstehung und Bedeutung des Konzepts 'Kirchengemeinschaft': Eine historische Skizze aus evangelischer Sicht," in **Communio Sanctorum: Einheit der Christen-Einheit der Kirche**, FS P.-W. Scheele, ed. Josef Schreiner & Klaus Wittstadt (Würzburg: Echter, 1988), especially pp. 219ff.

57. See the international Lutheran-Reformed dialogue, **Toward Church Fellowship** (1989).

58. For what follows, see the Leuenberg Agreement, especially §§29-34.

59. The nature of full communion is discussed in detail in the Report of the Anglican-Lutheran International Joint Working Group, **The Cold Ash Report** (1983), §§ 24-34.

60. Report of Anglican-Lutheran International Continuation Committee, **The Niagara Report**, Ch. 1.

# The Phrase "Full Communion" as a Statement of the Ecumenical Goal as Described in the Proposed Ecumenical Policy Statement of the ELCA

## A Dossier Prepared by Michael Root

**A.** The phrase *full communion* has been used in recent ecumenical dialogues involving Lutherans to refer to the ecumenical goal (emphasis on phrase *full communion* added throughout).

AMERICAN DIALOGUES

**1.** Lutheran-Reformed Dialogue Series III (1983): "1.8 Because God makes us all members of the holy catholic church by baptism, our churches are compelled to work together officially toward *full communion* in each other's baptism, Holy Communion, and ministry" (*An Invitation to Action: 2*).

**2.** *Lutheran-Episcopal Agreement* (1982): "5. Authorize and establish now a third series of Lutheran-Episcopal Dialogues for the discussion of any other outstanding questions that must be resolved before *full communion* (*communio in sacris*/altar and pulpit fellowship) can be established between the respective churches" (13).

EUROPEAN DIALOGUES

**3.** Anglican-Lutheran *Helsinki Report* (1982): "§62. We as a Commission believe that there are no longer any serious obstacles on the way towards the establishment of *full communion* between our two Churches." "§64. We therefore propose the following interim steps towards the full communion which we believe is now ultimately possible and which must also necessarily involve not only the complete interchangeability of our ministries, but also a visible sharing together in the *common life* of the Body of Christ" (Anglican-Lutheran European Commission: 29, emphasis in original).

**4.** Lutheran/Reformed *Leuenberg Accord* (1973): "§29. In the sense intended in this Agreement, *church fellowship* (*Kirchengemeinschaft*) means that, on the basis of the consensus they have reached in their understanding of the gospel, churches with different confessional positions accord each other fellowship in Word and sacrament, and strive for the fullest possible cooperation (*Gemeinsamkeit*) in witness and service to the world" (*An Invitation to Action*: 70).

(See discussion following in relation to the Lutheran/Catholic text *Ways to Community* about the translation of *Gemeinschaft* in this context. The most recent international Lutheran-Reformed dialogue statement (1988) explicitly refers to Leuenberg as a declaration of *full communion*. See *Toward Church Fellowship*, §29)

**5.** Lutheran/Reformed/Anglican *Meissen Paper* (1988): "§8. As the Churches grow together the understanding of the characteristics of full, visible unity become clearer. We can already claim together that full, visible unity must include:

– a common confession of the apostolic faith in word and life. . . .
– the sharing of one baptism, the celebrating of one Eucharist, and the service of a reconciled, common ministry. . . .
– *bonds of communion* (*Bande der Gemeinschaft*) which enable the church at every level to guard and interpret the apostolic faith, to take decisions, to teach authoritatively, to share goods and to bear effective witness in the world" (*Auf dem Weg zu sichtbarer Einheit*: 12).

## INTERNATIONAL DIALOGUES

**6.** Lutheran-Reformed *Toward Church Fellowship* 1989: "§79. In light of the discovery that nothing stands in the way of church fellowship, we urge Lutheran and Reformed churches throughout the world who are members of the Lutheran World Federation and the World Alliance of Reformed Churches to declare *full communion* with one another. By this we mean: §80. Acknowledging that the condemnations pronounced upon one another in former times are no longer regarded as applicable in today's situation. §81. Establishing full pulpit and altar/table fellowship, with the necessary mutual recognition of ministers ordained for Word and sacrament. §82. Committing themselves to growth in unity through new steps in church life and mission together" (Lutheran-Reformed Joint Commission, 28). [This last aspect is further spelled out in the following paragraphs.]

**7.** Lutheran/Anglican *Pullach Report* (1972): "§53. The goal should be full 'altar and pulpit fellowship' (*full communion*), including its acceptance by the individual members of the Churches, and structures that will encourage such fellowship and its acceptance" (H. Meyer: 20).

**8.** Lutheran/Anglican *The Cold Ash Report* (1983): "§24. We look forward to the day when *full communion* is established between Anglican and Lutheran churches."

"§25. By *full communion*, we here understand a relationship between two distinct churches or communions. Each maintains its own autonomy and recognizes the catholicity and apostolicity of the other, and each believes the other to hold the essentials of the Christian faith: (a) subject to such safeguards as ecclesial discipline may properly require, members of one body may receive the sacraments of the other; (b) subject to local invitation, bishops of one church may take part in the consecration of the bishops of the other, thus acknowledging the duty of mutual care and concern; (c) subject to church regulation, a bishop, pastor/priest or deacon of one ecclesial body may exercise liturgical functions in a congregation of the other body if invited to do so and also, when requested, pastoral care of the other's members; (d) it is also a necessary addition and complement that there should be recognized organs of regular consultation and communication, including episcopal collegiality, to express and strengthen the fellowship and enable common witness, life and service.

"§27. *Full communion* carries implications which go beyond sharing the same Eucharist. . . . To be in *full communion* implies a community of life, an exchange and a commitment to one another in respect of major decisions on questions of faith, order, and morals" (Anglican-Lutheran Joint Working Group: 13f).

**9.** Lutheran/Catholic *The Ministry in the Church* (1981): "§82. The precondition for such acceptance of *full church communion* (*vollen Kirchengemeinschaft*) is agreement in the confession of faith – which must also include a common understanding of the church's ministry – a common understanding of the sacraments, and fraternal fellowship in Christian and church life" (H. Meyer: 273).

**10.** Lutheran/Catholic *Ways to Community* [*Wege zur Gemeinschaft*] (1980): e.1. Fellowship (*Gemeinschaft*) of All Christians. "§92. The goal of *full communion* (*voller Gemeinschaft*) towards which Catholic and Lutheran Christians and churches are now moving together points far beyond itself. . . . But it also points far beyond itself in the sense that Roman Catholic-Lutheran fellowship (*Gemeinschaft*) is not yet the fellowship (*Gemeinschaft*) of all Christians" (H. Meyer: 236).

Here can be seen particularly clearly the translation question. The standard German term "Gemeinschaft" can be translated "fellowship," "communion," or "community." The standard French translation is "communion ecclesiale." The texts from the 1984 Budapest Assembly of the LWF consistently use the German "Gemeinschaft" and the English "communion" as equivalent. The English "fellowship" is also used, but only sparingly. The translators of the international Lutheran/Catholic texts have tended to use "communion" when a technical sense is implied, especially if the Latin term "communio" seems to be in the background, and "fellowship" at other times. Compare the English and German especially of *Facing Unity/Einheit vor Uns* §5f. The German version of the Lund 1952 definitions of ecumenical terms translates "full communion" as "volle Abendmahlsgemeinschaft." Thus, whether the Leuenberg Accord speaks of church fellowship or church communion is a question which can only be asked in English. [On the translation difficulties, see Brand 1988: 12f]

**B.** The phrase *full communion* corresponds to the description of church unity in the statement "The Unity We Seek," adopted by the LWF at its Budapest Assembly.

**11.** "The true unity of the church, which is the unity of the body of Christ and participates in the unity of the Father, Son, and Holy Spirit, is given in and through proclamation of the gospel in Word and sacrament. This unity is expressed as a communion in the common and, at the same time, multiform confession of one and the same apostolic faith. It is a communion in holy baptism and in the eucharistic meal, a communion in which the ministries exercised are recognized by all as expressions of the ministry instituted by Christ in his church. It is a communion where diversities contribute to fullness and are no longer barriers to unity. It is a committed fellowship, able to make common decisions and to act in common" (*Budapest 1984*: 175).

**C.** The phrase is widely used ecumenically to identify a particular understanding of the ecumenical goal.

## PART ONE: DIALOGUE STATEMENTS

**12.** United Church of Christ-Disciples of Christ (USA), *Vision Statement of the Ecumenical Partnership*, 1988: "As partners, we are working towards a time when our churches will be able to claim *full communion*, – a relationship characterized by a mutual recognition of baptism, full eucharistic fellowship, the mutual recognition of members and ordained ministers, a common commitment to confess the gospel of Christ by proclamation and service to the world, and common decision-making" (Cooper: 115).

**13.** Anglican-Roman Catholic, *Final Report of ARCIC 1*, Conclusion: "There are high expectations that significant initiatives will be boldly undertaken to deepen our reconciliation and lead us forward in the quest for the *full communion* to which we have been committed, in obedience to God, from the beginning of our dialogue" (H. Meyer: 116).

**14.** Anglican-Roman Catholic *Salvation and the Church* (1987): "The purpose of our dialogue is the restoration of *full ecclesial communion* between us," preface by co-chairman (Anglican-Roman Catholic Joint Commission: 612)

**15.** Methodist-Roman Catholic (international) *Towards a Statement on the Church* (1986): "§20: In obedience to him who will bring about this unity, we are committed to a vision that includes the goal of *full communion* in faith, mission and sacramental life" (Joint Commission: 247).

**16.** Anglican-Orthodox Steering Committee of Joint Doctrinal Discussions, July 1979 statement: "Our conversations are concerned with the search for a unity in faith. They are not negotiations for immediate *full communion*" (*Anglican-Orthodox Dialogue*: 3f).

## PART TWO: OTHER ECUMENICAL DOCUMENTS

**17.** World Conference of Faith and Order, Lund, 1952. Definitions of Terms. "*Full communion* (though the adjective need rarely be used): where churches in doctrinal agreement, or of the same confessional family, allow communicant members freely to communicate at the altars of each, and where there is freedom of ministers to officiate sacramentally in either Church (i.e., *Intercelebration*) e.g., the Orthodox, Anglican, Lutheran, and Reformed (Presbyterian) 'families' of Churches, respectively" (L. Vischer: 118)

**18.** *Beyond Intercommunion.* Faith and Order (1969): "§37. The first and most important of the terms proposed is *communion*. It indicates the goal to be achieved by the ecumenical movement. While this term describes the fellowship willed by Christ, the terms which follow refer to the anomalous situations of separation" (*Beyond Intercommunion*: 102).

**19.** Faith and Order Commission, WCC, *Bangalore 1978*: "It is its [the Faith and Order Commission's] constitutional task to contribute to the creation of conditions which will make it possible for the churches to enter into *full communion*. They will then recognize each other's ministries; they will share the bread and the cup of their Lord; they will acknowledge each other as belonging to the body of Christ in all places and at all times; they will proclaim together the Gospel to the world; they will serve the needs of humankind in mutual trust and dedication; and for these ends they will plan and take decisions together in assemblies constituted by authorized representatives wherever this is required" (Faith and Order 1978: 237).

**20.** Lambeth Conference 1968: "*Full communion* involves mutual recognition of ministers and members (e.g., the relationship between Churches of the Anglican communion" (Lambeth Conference: 125).

**21.** *The Emmaus Report* (Anglican international ecumenical consultation in preparation for Lambeth Conference) 1987: "The phrase '*full communion*'. . . appears to have different emphases in the various international theological dialogues with different denominations. All seem to be agreed that it means: (a) sharing a common essential faith; (b) full interchangeability of ministry and membership, including the participation of bishops of one Church in the consecration of bishops in the other. Most agree: (c) that it should include regular organs of consultation and common action" (*The Emmaus Report*: 33).

**D.** The phrase *full communion* has come to have a sufficiently stable meaning to communicate our ecumenical goal.

If one compares the descriptions of full communion in the selections given above, particularly in the UCC-Disciples of Christ Vision Statement (12.), *The Emmaus Report* (21.), *The Cold Ash Report* (8.), and the Bangalore Faith and Order Statement (19.), one can see a broad agreement on the meaning of *full communion*. *Full communion* implies more than declarations of mutual acceptability, but less than organizational merger. It involves unity in the confession of faith, mutual acceptability of members and ordained ministers, some forms of common life and witness, and structure for consultation and decision making in relation at least to common activities.

If there is an ambiguity in the meaning of the phrase, it is in relation to such forms of common decision making. The exact form such common decision making should take is still a matter of discussion. At the very least, common actions will require forms of common decision making in relation to such common actions. The open question is: if no Christian community is the Church in isolation from the rest of the Church, in decisions about fundamental matters, to what degree should decisions be made independently and to what degree in relation to other communities? There is no agreed answer to this question as yet. The concept *full communion* only implies the general principle that life together implies some forms of common decision making.

The definition of *full communion* in the proposed ELCA statement follows the ecumenical consensus on the meaning of the term.

**E.** Does the phrase *full communion* contain hidden meanings, such as episcopal succession, or imply some bias toward particular traditions?

A survey of the selections shows a relatively consistent meaning. There seems no ground to assume that the phrase conceals some hidden meaning. In particular, the phrase implies nothing about the necessity or advisability of episcopal succession, as the above selections show. If churches are to be in *full communion*, each must be open to the other's ordained ministry. Thus, churches in *full communion* must reach a minimal agreement on what constitutes an acceptable ordained ministry. But the concept *full communion* implies nothing about what such an agreement may or may not imply about the structure of that ministry. Such non-episcopal churches as the United Church of Christ and the Disciples of Christ (12.) can adopt the phrase *full communion* to describe their ecumenical goal without in any way adopting even the sort of episcopacy practiced by the ELCA, not to mention episcopal succession.

The phrase has been used both by the ecumenical movement as a whole and by individual churches with a variety of backgrounds. There seems no ground for assuming that the term implies some bias toward a particular tradition. Some people seem to think that the term has a somewhat Anglican sound. Nevertheless, as recently as 1930, the term was still not in common use among Anglicans. The ecumenical resolutions of the 1930 Lambeth Conference still do not use the term (see Bell: 1-7).

**F.** The only comprehensive study of ecumenical terminology carried out by a Lutheran agency recommended the term *full communion* for the ecumenical goal.

In 1963, the Theology Commission of the LWF sponsored essays on "altar fellowship [*Abendmahlsgemeinschaft*]" in German, Scandinavian, and North American Lutheranism, published in English under the title *Church in Fellowship: Pulpit and Altar Fellowship Among Lutherans* [German edition, *Kirche und Abendmahl. Studien und Dokumentation zur Frage der Abendmahlsgemeinschaft im Luthertum*]. Vilmos Vajta, at that time director of LWF's Theology Department, added a systematic essay on "The Unity of The Church and Holy Communion." The second section of the essay dealt with terminology. After noting the difficulty of clarifying the terminology, he concluded: "An attempt should at least be made, based on the new approach made by the Conference on Faith and Order at Lund in 1952." The concept he recommends for full community of faith is the first defined by Lund, *full communion*, which is translated into German as "Volle Abendmahlsgemeinschaft." While noting some difficulties with the phrase, he states in a sentence italicized in the German original: "We should retain the concept of fellowship (*communio*) for full fellowship between the churches" (226). The German original of the sentence reads: "Wir sollten den Begriff Communio/Gemeinschaft für die volle Kirchengemeinschaft bestehen lassen." The German original and the fact that he is recommending adopting the phrase from Lund makes clear that what Vajta is recommending is the phrase *full communion*. Unfortunately, the English translation of the German translation of Lund's terminology obscures this fact.

He states that this concept should be adopted because it "corresponds to the New Testament usage." He understands the meaning of *full communion* in line with the discussion above: "This concept must not lose its force through modulations. It should rather denote full fellowship in the exercise of ministry, i.e., in preaching and in administering both the sacraments. This fellowship, however, should also be a fellowship of prayer and practice" (226).

G. Would "fellowship" or "altar and pulpit fellowship" be better terms to describe our ecumenical goal?

## PART ONE: "FELLOWSHIP" OR "FULL FELLOWSHIP"

Between "fellowship" and "communion" there is, in the abstract, little difference, unless one means by "fellowship" something different than "communion." "Fellowship" may be seen as not gender-inclusive. Werner Elert repeated doubts about the phrase "fellowship" [*Gemeinschaft*] as a modern equivalent for the Latin *communio* and Greek *koinonia* since "fellowship" seemed to refer only to our relations one to another, rather than to that reality beyond us both, in which we are one (Elert: 4f).

Perhaps decisive should be the wide ecumenical usage of *full communion* rather than "fellowship" or "full fellowship" to describe the sort of goal elaborated by the Policy Statement.

## PART TWO: "ALTAR AND PULPIT FELLOWSHIP"

Do the phrases "*full communion*" and "[full] altar and pulpit fellowship" have the same meaning?

On occasion, the terms have been treated as synonymous. The terms are equated in the 1982 *Lutheran-Episcopal Agreement* (2.) and the *Pullach Report* (7.). In his contribution to the 1963 LWF Theology Commission study of altar fellowship, Fred W. Meuser used the term *full communion* as a synonym for "full altar and pulpit fellowship" (e.g., pp. 17, 63).

Nevertheless, one can see in the documents a tendency to understand *full communion* more inclusively than "altar and pulpit fellowship." That altar and pulpit fellowship is only one aspect of *full communion* is explicit in the 1989 Lutheran-Reformed Statement *Toward Church Fellowship* (6.). Here, "altar and pulpit fellowship" presumably refers to mutual admission to each other's altars and openness to pastors of the other church both preaching and presiding at the Eucharist within one's own church. *Full communion* is the term for the wider total fellowship in witness and life to which churches which are one are called. Such a differentiation can be found in Lutheran documents. In the 1925 Minneapolis Theses of the churches which came to form the American Lutheran Conference, "altar and pulpit fellowship" is identified as one element of a more inclusive "church fellowship."

> **22**. Section III. ". . . church fellowship, that is, mutual recognition, altar and pulpit fellowship, and eventually cooperation in the strictly essential work of the church, presupposes unanimity in the pure doctrine of the Gospel and of the confession of the same in word and deed" (Wolf: 146).

Similar is the 1984 LWF "Statement on the Self-Understanding and Task of the LWF," adopted by the Budapest Assembly.

> **23**. "This Lutheran communion of churches finds its visible expression in pulpit and altar fellowship, in common witness and service, in the joint fulfillment of the missionary task, and in openness to ecumenical cooperation, dialog, and community" (*Budapest 1984: 176*).

Again, pulpit and altar fellowship is taken to be one aspect of a larger common life and witness. In his study *Toward a Lutheran Communion: Pulpit and Altar Fellowship*, Eugene Brand of the LWF reached a similar conclusion: "Pulpit and altar fellowship are essential, even basic, to communio, but communio (koinonia) is both broader and deeper" (73).

It would thus appear that "pulpit and altar fellowship" is taken to refer only to fellowship realized in reciprocal admission to the Lord's Supper and mutual availability of ordained ministers to preach and preside at the Supper in either church. One should note that one could take the phrase to mean a fellowship which centered on these relations, but which took in also the wider common witness and life referred to by *full communion*. Nevertheless, at the very least it is unclear whether "altar and pulpit fellowship" refers also to such a wider common life. On the whole, the more recent texts seem to envisage "altar and pulpit fellowship" as having a more narrow meaning and *full communion* as referring to a more inclusive common life and witness.

If the last sentence is accurate, then the choice between *full communion* and "altar and pulpit fellowship" as descriptions of the ecumenical goal can be explained in terms of the six aspects of *full communion* in the proposed statement *Ecumenism: The Vision of the Evangelical Lutheran Church in America*.

If our ecumenical goal is *full communion*, then we are called to realize with churches with whom we are one in Word and sacrament all six of the listed aspects.

If our ecumenical goal is "altar and pulpit fellowship," then we are called to realize with churches with whom we are one in Word and sacrament only aspects 1, 2, 3, and 6, with the understanding that the "common confessing" of aspect 1 refers only to our each independently confessing the faith, not to any joint action.

Most simply then, the choice between *full communion* and "altar and pulpit fellowship" as statements of our ecumenical goal is this: when we find ourselves one in agreement over the proclamation of the Word and celebration of the sacraments with another church, are we then called to: (1) *mutual openness* to each other's laity and clergy in preaching and sacrament, or (2) mutual openness *and common witness and life*, including means of common decision making related at least to that common witness and life.

If you agree with (1), then you should adopt "altar and pulpit fellowship" as the term for our ecumenical goal.

If you agree with (2), then you should adopt *full communion* as the term for our ecumenical goal.

If you think that the ecumenical goal involves the disappearance of distinct church organizations, then you should adopt some such term as "organic union" for the ecumenical goal.

The quotations from Lutheran ecumenical documents given above clearly assume that altar and pulpit fellowship is one aspect of our ecumenical goal, but that the unity of the church also calls us to forms of common life and witness. Note, in particular, the reference to "common life" in the *Helsinki Report* (3.), the call for the "fullest possible cooperation in witness and service" in the *Leuenberg Accord* (4.), the comprehensive description of "full, visible unity" in the *Meissen Paper* (5.), the description of *full communion* in *Toward Church Fellowship* (6.) and in *The Cold Ash Report* (8.), the call for "fraternal fellowship in Christian and church life" in the international Lutheran-Catholic *Ministry* statement (9.), and the description of church unity adopted by the LWF in its 1984 statement "The Unity We Seek" (10.). The assumption of Lutheran ecumenical efforts has clearly been that we are seeking not just altar and pulpit fellowship with other churches, but also the sort of wider common witness and life referred to with the phrase *full communion*.

The Constitution of the ELCA states that:

> **24.** "(4.02.) To participate in God's mission, this church shall: f. Manifest the unity given to the people of God by living together in the love of Christ

and *by joining with other Christians in prayer and action* to express and preserve the unity which the Spirit gives."

"(4.03.) To fulfill these purposes, this church shall: e. Foster Christian unity by participating in ecumenical activities, contributing its witness and work and *cooperating with other churches* which confess God the Father, Son, and Holy Spirit."

It would appear that the ELCA is constitutionally committed to seek more than mere altar and pulpit fellowship with other churches, but also the sort of fuller cooperation and joint prayer and action that ecumenically has come to be referred to as full communion.

## APPENDIX 3 BIBLIOGRAPHY

Anglican-Lutheran European Commission. *Anglican-Lutheran Dialogue: Helsinki Report 1982*. London: SPCK, 1983.

Anglican-Lutheran Joint Working Group. *Anglican-Lutheran Revelations: The Cold Ash Report*. London: Anglican Consultative Council; Geneva: Lutheran World Federation, 1983.

*Anglican-Orthodox Dialogue: The Dublin Agreed Statement 1984*. London: SPCK, 1984.

Anglican-Roman Catholic Joint Commission, "Salvation and the Church: ARCIC II," *Origins*, 16 (1987):611-16.

*Auf dem Weg zu sichtbarer Einheit: eine gemeinsame Feststellung*. Kirche von England, Bund der Evangelischen Kirchen in der Deutschen Demokratischen Republik, Evangelische Kirche in Deutschland. Berlin and Hannover, 1988.

Bell, G. K. A. *Documents of Christian Unity: Third Series, 1930-48*. London: Oxford University Press, 1948.

*"Beyond Intercommunion: On the Way to Communion in the Eucharist*. A study paper of the Commission on Faith and Order." *Study Encounter* 5 (1969):94-114.

Brand, Eugene L., *Toward a Lutheran Communion: Pulpit and Altar Fellowship*. LWF Report no. 26 (Geneva: Lutheran World Federation, 1988).

*Budapest 1984: "In Christ—Hope for the World."* Official Proceedings of the Seventh Assembly of the Lutheran World Federation. *LWF Report* nos. 19/20 (1985).

Cooper, Charles W., Jr. "New Ecumenical Partnership of The United Church of Christ and Disciples of Christ." *Ecumenical Trends* 17 (1988):113-15.

Elert, Werner. *Eucharist and Church Fellowship in the First Four Centuries*. Translated by N. E. Nagel. St. Louis: Concordia Publishing House, 1966.

*The Emmaus Report*: A Report of the Anglican Ecumenical Consultation that took place at the Emmaus Retreat Centre, West Wickham, Kent, England 27, January-2 February 1987 in preparation for ACC-7, Singapore, 1987 and The Lambeth Conference 1988. London: Church House Publishing, 1987.

Faith and Order Commission, World Council of Churches. *Bangalore 1978: Sharing in One Hope*. Reports and Documents from the Meeting of the Faith and Order

Commission, 15-30 August, 1978, Bangalore, India. Geneva: World Council of Churches, 1978.

*An Invitation to Action: A Study of Ministry, Sacraments, and Recognition. The Lutheran-Reformed Dialogue Series III, 1981-1983.* James E. Andrews and Joseph A. Burgess, eds. Philadelphia: Fortress Press, 1984.

Joint Commission between the Roman Catholic Church and the World Methodist Council. "Towards a Statement on the Church: Report of the Joint Commission between the Roman Catholic Church and the World Methodist Council, 1982-1986 (Fourth Series)." *One in Christ* 22 (1986):241-59.

*Lambeth Conference 1968: Resolutions and Reports.* London: SPCK; New York: Seabury, 1968.

*Lutheran-Episcopal Agreement: Commentary and Guidelines.* New York: Division for World Mission and Ecumenism, Lutheran Church in America, 1983.

Lutheran-Reformed Joint Commission. *Toward Church Fellowship.* Geneva: Lutheran World Federation and World Alliance of Reformed Churches, 1989.

Meuser, Fred W. "Pulpit and Altar Fellowship Among Lutherans in America" in *Church in Fellowship: Pulpit and Altar Fellowship Among Lutherans*, ed. Vilmos Vajta, 1-72. Minneapolis: Augsburg, 1963.

Meyer, Harding and Lukas Vischer, eds. *Growth in Agreement: Reports and Agreed Statements of Ecumenical Conversations on a World Level.* New York: Paulist Press; Geneva: World Council of Churches, 1984.

Vajta, Vilmos. "The Unity of the Church and Holy Communion" in *Church in Fellowship: Pulpit and Altar Fellowship Among Lutherans*, ed. Vilmos Vatja, 222-72. Minneapolis: Augsburg, 1963.

Vischer, Lukas, ed. *A Documentary History of the Faith and Order Movement 1927-1963.* St. Louis: Bethany Press, 1963.

Wolf, Richard C. *Documents of Lutheran Unity in America.* Philadelphia: Fortress Press, 1966.

# General Bibliography

In addition to the volumes listed below, see the bibliographies in Appendix 1 and Appendix 3.

Althaus, Paul. *The Theology of Martin Luther*. Translated by Robert C. Schultz. Philadelphia: Fortress Press, 1966.

Anderson, H.G., T. Austin Murphy, and Joseph A. Burgess, eds. *Justification by Faith: Lutherans and Catholics in Dialogue VII*. Minneapolis: Augsburg, 1985.

Andrews, James E. and Joseph A. Burgess, eds. *An Invitation to Action: The Lutheran Reformed Dialogue, Series III, 1981-1983*. Philadelphia: Fortress Press, 1985.

*Anglican-Lutheran Dialogue*. The Report of the Anglican-Lutheran European Commission. London: SPCK, 1982.

Bachmann, E. Theodore. *The Ecumenical Involvement of the LCA Predecessor Bodies: A Brief History 1900-1962*. Rev. 2d ed. New York: Division for World Mission and Ecumenism, Lutheran Church in America, 1983.

*Baptism, Eucharist and Ministry* (BEM). Faith and Order Paper no. 111. Geneva: World Council of Churches, 1982.

*Die Bekenntnisschriften der evangelisch-lutherischen Kirche*. 6., durchgesehene Auflage. Göttingen: Vandenhoeck & Ruprecht, 1967.

Bergendoff, Conrad. *The Church of the Lutheran Reformation: A Historical Survey of Lutheranism*. St. Louis: Concordia Publishing House, 1967.

"The Bilateral Consultations Between the Roman Catholic Church in the United States and Other Christian Communions (1972-1979)." In *Catholic Theological Society of America Annual Report*. Vol. 34. 253-85. Mahwah, NJ: Catholic Theological Society of America, 1980.

Birmelé, André, ed. *Konkordie und Kirchengemeinschaft: reformatorischer Kirchen im Europa der Gegenwart.* Vol. 2, *Ökumenische Perspektiven.* Frankfurt: Verlag Otto Lembeck and Verlag Josef Knecht, 1973.

———. "Nos différences ecclésiales: leur enjeu dans la recherche de l'unité." In *Consensus oecuménique et différence fondamentale.* Comité mixte catholique-protestant en France. 29-44. Paris: Le Centurion, 1987.

———. *Le salut en Jésus Christ dans les dialogues œcuméniques.* Paris: Les Éditions du Cerf, 1986.

Braaten, Carl. *Justification: The Article by Which the Church Stands or Falls.* Minneapolis: Fortress Press, 1990.

———. *Principles of Lutheran Theology.* Philadelphia: Fortress Press, 1983.

——— and Robert W. Jenson. *Christian Dogmatics.* 2 vols. Philadelphia: Fortress Press, 1984.

Brand, Eugene L. *Toward a Lutheran Communion: Pulpit and Altar Fellowship,* LWF Report no. 26. Geneva: Lutheran World Federation, 1988.

Brown, Raymond E., Karl P. Donfried, Joseph A. Fitzmyer, and John Reumann, eds. *Mary in the New Testament: A Collaborative Assessment by Protestant and Roman Catholic Scholars.* Sponsored by the United States Lutheran-Roman Catholic Dialogue. Philadelphia: Fortress Press; New York: Paulist Press, 1978.

Chemnitz, Martin. *Justification: The Chief Article of Christian Doctrine as Expounded in "Loci Theologici."* Translated by J.A.O. Preus. St. Louis: Concordia Publishing House, 1985.

———. *The Lord's Supper.* Translated by J.A.O. Preus. St. Louis: Concordia Publishing House, 1979.

*Christology, The Lord's Supper and Its Observance in the Church.* A Reexamination of Lutheran and Reformed Traditions - II. N.p. North American Area of the World Alliance of Reformed Churches Holding the Presbyterian Order and the U.S.A. National Committee of the Lutheran World Federation, 1964.

*The Church: Community of Grace.* The Lutheran-Methodist Dialogue 1979-1984. Geneva: Lutheran World Federation; Lake Junaluska, NC: World Methodist Council, 1984.

Ebeling, Gerhard. *The Problem of Historicity.* Translated by Grover Foley. Philadelphia: Fortress Press, 1967.

*Ecumenical Relations of the Lutheran World Federation.* Report of the Working Group on the Interrelations Between Various Bilateral Dialogues. Geneva: Lutheran World Federation, 1977.

*Ecumenical Methodology: Documentation Report.* Geneva: Lutheran World Federation, 1978.

Empie, Paul, and James I. McCord, eds. *Marburg Revisited: A Reexamination of Lutheran and Reformed Traditions.* Minneapolis: Augsburg, 1966.

———, T. Austin Murphy, and Joseph A. Burgess, eds. *Teaching Authority & Infallibility in the Church: Lutherans and Catholics in Dialogue VI.* Minneapolis: Augsburg, 1980.

*Ethics and Ethos: Summaries and Comments.* A Reexamination of Lutheran and Reformed Traditions - IV. N.p. North American Area of the World Alliance of Reformed Churches Holding the Presbyterian Order and the U.S.A. National Committee of the Lutheran World Federation, 1966.

*The Eucharist.* Lutheran/Roman Catholic Joint Commission. Geneva: Lutheran World Federation, 1980.

*Facing Unity: Models, Forms and Phases of Catholic-Lutheran Fellowship.* Roman Catholic/Lutheran Joint Commission. Geneva: Lutheran World Federation, 1985.

Flesner, Dorris A. *American Lutherans Help Shape World Council: The Role of the Lutheran Churches of America in the Formation of the World Council of Churches.* Lutheran Historical Conference Publication no. 2. Dubuque, IA: Wm. C. Brown Co., 1981.

Forde, Gerhard O. "Justification by Faith Alone." *Dialog* 27 (Fall 1988):260-67.

———. *Where God Meets Man: Luther's Down-to-Earth Approach to the Gospel.* Minneapolis: Augsburg, 1972.

Forell, George Wolfgang, and James F. McCue, eds. *Confessing One Faith: A Joint Commentary on the Augsburg Confession by Lutheran and Catholic Theologians.* Minneapolis: Augsburg, 1982.

*From Budapest to Curitiba*, LWF Report no. 27. Geneva: Lutheran World Federation, 1989.

"The Gospel and the Church." Report of the Joint Lutheran/Roman Catholic Study Commission. LWF Report no. 3. Geneva: Lutheran World Federation, 1972.

Gritsch, Eric W., and Robert W. Jenson. *Lutheranism: The Theological Movement and Its Confessional Writings.* Philadelphia: Fortress Press, 1976.

Hooft, W.A. Visser't, ed. *Amsterdam.* London: SCM Press, 1949.

*Justification and Sanctification; Liturgy and Ethics; Creation and Redemption; Law and Gospel.* A Reexamination of Lutheran and Reformed Traditions - III. N.p. North American Area of the World Alliance of Reformed Churches Holding the Presbyterian Order and the U.S.A. National Committee of the Lutheran World Federation, 1965.

*Justification by Faith: Lutherans and Catholics in Dialogue VII.* Edited by H. George Anderson, T. Austin Murphy, and Joseph A. Burgess. Minneapolis: Augsburg, 1985.

Küng, Hans. *The Church.* Translated by Ray and Rosaleen Ockenden. London: Burns & Oates Limited, 1967.

Lienhard, Marc. *Lutherische-Reformierte Kirchengemeinschaft Heute.* Vol. 2, Ökumenische Perspektiven. Frankfurt: Verlag Otto Lembeck and Verlag Josef Knecht, 1973.

Lull, Timothy F. "The Doctrine of Justification Today." *Dialog* 27 (Fall 1988): 250-59.

Luther, Martin. *Career of the Reformer I.* Edited by Harold J. Grimm. Vol. 31, *Luther's Works.* Philadelphia: Fortress Press, 1957.

———. *Career of the Reformer II.* Edited by George W. Forell. Vol. 32, *Luther's Works.* Philadelphia: Fortress Press, 1958.

———. *Church and Ministry I.* Edited by Eric W. Gritsch. Vol. 39, *Luther's Works.* Philadelphia: Fortress Press, 1970.

———. *First Lectures on the Psalms II: Psalms 76-126.* Edited by Hilton C. Oswald. Vol. 11, *Luther's Works.* St. Louis: Concordia, 1976.

———. *Lectures on Genesis: Chapters 6-14.* Edited by Jaroslav Pelikan. Vol. 2, *Luther's Works.* St. Louis: Concordia, 1960.

———. *Lectures on Genesis: Chapters 15-20.* Edited by Jaroslav Pelikan. Vol. 3, *Luther's Works.* St. Louis: Concordia, 1961.

———. *Lectures on Isaiah: Chapters 40-66.* Edited by Hilton C. Oswald. Vol. 17, *Luther's Works.* St. Louis: Concordia, 1972.

———. *Selected Psalms II.* Edited by Jaroslav Pelikan. Vol. 13, *Luther's Works.* St. Louis: Concordia, 1956.

———. *Sermons II.* Edited by Hans J. Hillerbrand. Vol. 52, *Luther's Works.* Philadelphia: Fortress Press, 1974.

———. *Sermons on the Gospel of St. John: Chapters 1-4.* Edited by Jaroslav Pelikan. Vol. 13, *Luther's Works.* St. Louis: Concordia, 1956.

———. *Word and Sacrament.* Abdel Ross Wentz. Vol. 36, *Luther's Works.* Philadelphia: Fortress Press, 1959.

*The Lutheran-Episcopal Agreement: Commentary and Guidelines.* New York: Lutheran Church in America, 1983.

*The Lutheran-Episcopal Dialogue: A Progress Report.* Cincinnati: Forward Movement Publications, 1973.

Martensen, Daniel F. *The Federation and the World Council of Churches.* LWF Report no. 3. Geneva: Lutheran World Federation, 1978.

Maurer, Wilhelm. *Historical Commentary on the Augsburg Confession.* Translated by H. George Anderson. Philadelphia: Fortress Press, 1986.

*Meaning and Practice of the Lord's Supper.* Edited by Helmut T. Lehmann. Philadelphia: Muhlenberg Press, 1961.

Meyer, Harding. "The LWF and Its Role in the Ecumenical Movement." *Lutheran World* 20.1 (1973):19.

———, ed. *Lutheran/Roman Catholic Discussion on the Augsburg Confession: Documents - 1977-1981.* LWF Report no. 10. Geneva: Lutheran World Federation, 1982.

——— and Lucas Vischer, eds. *Growth in Agreement: Reports and Agreed Statements of Ecumenical Conversations on a World Level.* Faith and Order Paper no. 108. New York: Paulist Press, 1984.

*The Ministry and the Church*. Roman Catholic/Lutheran Joint Commission. Geneva: Lutheran World Federation, 1982.

Nelson, E. Clifford. *Lutheranism in North America 1914-1970*. Minneapolis: Augsburg, 1972.

*The Niagara Report: Report of the Anglican-Lutheran Consultation on Episcope*. London: Anglican Consultative Council; Geneva: Lutheran World Federation, 1968.

Pannenberg, Wolfhart. *The Apostles' Creed: In Light of Today's Questions*. Translated by Margaret Kohl. Philadelphia: Westminster Press, 1975.

Pelikan, Jaroslav. *The Riddle of Roman Catholicism*. New York and Nashville: Abingdon Press, 1959.

——. *Reformation of Church and Dogma (1300-1700)*. Vol. 4, *The Christian Tradition: A History of the Development of Doctrine*. Chicago: University of Chicago Press, 1984.

Piepkorn, Arthur Carl. *Protestant Denominations*. Vol. 2, *Profiles in Belief: The Religious Bodies of the United States and Canada*. San Francisco: Harper & Row, 1978.

Quanbeck, Warren A. *Search for Understanding: Lutheran Conversations with Reformed, Anglican, and Roman Catholic Churches*. Minneapolis: Augsburg, 1972.

*The Report of the Lutheran-Episcopal Dialogue Second Series 1976-1980*. Cincinnati: Forward Movement Publications, 1981.

Reumann, John. "Lutherans in Dialogue." In vol. 18, *New Catholic Encyclopedia: Supplement 1978-1988*, 271-74. Palatine, IL: Jack Heraty & Assoc. in association with the Catholic University, Washington, D.C., 1989.

Reumann, John, et al. *"Righteousness" in the New Testament: Justification in the United States*. Lutheran-Roman Catholic Dialogue. Philadelphia: Fortress Press, 1982.

Rusch, William G. *Ecumenism: A Movement Toward Church Unity*. Philadelphia: Fortress Press, 1985.

Rusch, William G., and Daniel F. Martensen. *The Leuenberg Agreement and Lutheran-Reformed Relationships: Evaluations by North American and European Theologians*. Minneapolis: Augsburg, 1989.

Schieffer, Elisabeth. *Von Schauenburg nach Leuenberg: Entstehung und Bedeutung der Konkordie reformatorischer Kirchen in Europa*. Paderborn: Verlag Bonifatius-Druckerei, 1983.

Schlink, Edmund. *Theology of the Lutheran Confessions*. Translated by Paul F. Koehneke and Herbert J.A. Bouman. Philadelphia: Muhlenberg Press, 1961.

Seils, Michael. *Lutheran Convergence?* LWF Report no. 25. Geneva: Lutheran World Federation, 1988.

Tappert, Theodore G., trans. and ed. *The Book of Concord: The Confessions of the Evangelical Lutheran Church*. Philadelphia: Fortress Press, 1959.

Tavard, George H. *Justification: An Ecumenical Study*. New York: Paulist Press, 1983.

*Toward Church Fellowship*. Report of the Commission of the Lutheran World Federation and the World Alliance. Geneva: Lutheran World Federation, 1989.

Vajta, Vilmos, ed. *Confessio Augustana 1530-1980: Commemoration and Self-Examination.* LWF Report no. 9. Geneva: Lutheran World Federation, 1980.

——, ed. *The Gospel as History.* Philadelphia: Fortress Press, 1975.

*Ways to Community.* Common Statement by the Roman Catholic/Lutheran Joint Commission. Geneva: Lutheran World Federation, 1981.

Wentz, Abdel Ross. *Lutheran Churches and the Modern Ecumenical Movement.* In *World Lutheranism of Today: A Tribute to Anders Nygren.* Stockholm: Svenska Kyrkans Diakonistyrelses Bokförlag, 1950.

Wingren, Gustaf. *Gospel and Church.* Translated by Ross MacKenzie. Philadelphia: Fortress Press, 1964.